A SECOND GENERATION UNITED NATIONS

As the United Nations moves beyond its fiftieth anniversary into the new millennium, it is faced with a new global system fraught with political and economic tensions that can no longer be handled with models that defined the organization when it was founded in 1945.

An innovative vision for a restructuring of the United Nations, this book offers an insider's look at how the UN can respond more effectively to the challenges of the future in an age of globalization. Guido de Marco and Michael Bartolo, seasoned veterans of the United Nations, provide valuable policy recommendations involving a combination of political will, relevance, and efficiency in the coming years.

Analysing the roles of major United Nations organs such as the General Assembly, the Trusteeship Council, the Economic and Social Council (ECOSOC), the Security Council and the Secretariat, de Marco and Bartolo call for a more relevant and strengthened General Assembly as the truly representative organ of the United Nations, where all Member States of the Organization are permanent Members. They also call for a decentralization of United Nations activities, and for building stronger relationships with established regional entities and the Bretton Woods institutions.

The proposals made here open up an important area of discussion beyond the confines of the United Nations as international policymakers seek peace and stability in the post-Cold War world.

THE AUTHORS

Guido de Marco has been the President of Malte since April 1999. During his political career, he served as Deputy Prime Minister and Minister of Foreign Affairs of Malta, and was also Leader of the House of Representatives. In 1990, Professor de Marco was elected President of the 45th Session of the United Nations General Assembly. It was principally due to his efforts that, during this session, the question of revitalization of the United Nations was brought again onto the agenda. Professor de Marco is a professor of Criminal Law at the University of Malta. He is a Companion of the Order of Merit of Malta, and his previous publications include *A Presidency with a Purpose; Malta's Foreign Policy in the Nineties,* and numerous articles in international journals.

Michael Bartolo is the Ambassador of Malta to the United Nations and other international organizations in Geneva and Vienna. In addition to serving as principal advisor to Professor de Marco, when he was President of the United Nations General Assembly, Dr Bartolo, who recently retired from the United Nations, worked for 26 years in the Secretariat of the United Nations in New York, beginning in early 1968 when the United Nations Secretariat was engaged in restructuring. He left the United Nations in July 1994 when the United Nations Secretariat was still undergoing restructuring. His previous publications include, *Limitations of UN Technical Assistance* and, as co-author, the chapter on Malta in *Mediterranean Europe and the Common Market.*

At the time of going to press, a new government was elected in Malta. Therefore any references in the book to the policies and positions of the Government of Malta refer to the policies and positions of the previous government.

A SECOND GENERATION UNITED NATIONS

FOR PEACE IN FREEDOM IN THE 21ST CENTURY

Guido de Marco and Michael Bartolo

Routledge
Taylor & Francis Group

LONDON AND NEW YORK

First published in 1997 by
Kegan Paul International

This edition first published in 2009 by
Routledge
2 Park Square, Milton Park, Abingdon, Oxon, OX14 4RN

Simultaneously published in the USA and Canada
by Routledge
270 Madison Avenue, New York, NY 10016

Routledge is an imprint of the Taylor & Francis Group, an informa business

© Guido de Marco and Michael Bartolo, 1997

Transferred to Digital Printing 2009

British Library Cataloguing in Publication Data
A catalogue record for this book is available from the British Library

ISBN 10: 0-7103-0558-3 (hbk)
ISBN 13: 978-0-7103-0558-9 (hbk)

Publisher's Note
The publisher has gone to great lengths to ensure the quality of this reprint
but points out that some imperfections in the original copies may be
apparent. The publisher has made every effort to contact original copyright
holders and would welcome correspondence from those they have been
unable to trace.

AUTHORS' NOTE

The authors wish to acknowledge the valuable assistance of Ms Nadia Burger, Mr Emanuel Spiry and Mr Patrick Cirillo, graduate students at the Institute of Graduate Studies of the University of Geneva. Thanks are also due to many others, including Dr Joseph Cassar and Mr Carl Freeman, for their helpful suggestions.

The views expressed in this book are those of the authors, and although these may coincide to a large extent with the official views of the Maltese Government, the authors alone assume responsibility for the contents of the book and for any errors it may contain.

To those who have served the United Nations
and in particular to those
who in defending its ideals lost their lives.

FOREWORD

Dr Vladimir Petrovsky, *United Nations Under-Secretary-General, Director-General of the United Nations Office at Geneva*

It is indeed a great honour and pleasure to write the foreword to what I believe is a timely and interesting book aimed at making the UN more relevant, focused and efficient, which should be the strategic aim of any reform proposals.

As an academician, I wrote my first book on diplomacy. In the past, diplomacy was always overshadowed by other subjects, in the nineteenth century by the study of international relations, in this century by the studies of foreign policy.

Meanwhile, diplomacy is a very special subject which deals with the art and science of negotiations. Diplomacy is an important instrument of influence in international affairs, and Malta provides a very convincing example of this. In the UN and the OSCE one can trace the very specific diplomatic style of Malta. Professor de Marco's presidency of the forty-fifth session of the UN General Assembly, the most representative forum of international organizations, has become a landmark in the process of renewal of the unique body of multilateral diplomacy. In the words of Dr de Marco it was a starting point, for the UN of the second generation.

The 50th Anniversary of the United Nations provides time for reflection on the UN, and on the reforms needed to adapt our global Organization to the new political environment.

The activities of the world Organization are now widely discussed among politicians, the mass media, and the public at large. Opinions expressed are rather different, ranging from idealizing the world Organization, to diminishing its role in contemporary international politics, and sometimes even accusing it of being involved in some sort of global conspiracy. As pointed out by the authors of this book it is not surprising that with so many diverse points of view there is no lack of proposals on how to reform the Organization.

I agree that first of all, the reform of the UN should be put into a broader international context. What we are facing today is not a change from a cold war to a post-cold war system. This change is only the visible part of the iceberg. In reality we face the change of the civilizational paradigm which affects not only the role of the States, but also of human beings and their interrelation. At least in politico-economic spheres we can see the contours not of a single polar, but rather a multi-polar world with new centres of economic might. In this period of transition, which is taking place in an ever-growing interdependent world, the UN serves as a kind of safety net, minimizing the damaging effect of the changes.

Secondly, during this transitional period we need a step-by-step, rather than a radical approach to reform. There is a French saying: '*on ne change pas de cheval au milieu du gué*'. Reform should be considered not as a one-act play, but rather as an evolutionary process which should be started by awakening the UN Charter which still reminds me of 'the sleeping beauty'. The only difference from the fairy tale is that in order to be awakened, this 'sleeping beauty' needs a kiss, not from one, but from 185 princes.

Thirdly, reform needs its own strategy – making the UN more relevant, more focused, more efficient and more cost effective. I am therefore very pleased to see the question of relevance as a predominant feature of this book. More relevance means the ability of the UN to serve as a focal point to identify new global issues and as a centre of agreed action of Member States. More efforts are needed today to search for solutions to challenges, not only in the traditional military-political and social-economic spheres, but also in the sphere of human security. New challenges can be identified including the proliferation of weapons, and in particular those of mass destruction, terrorism, organized crime, the criminalization of societies and environmental degradation and population growth. Relevance also demands further democratization of the UN.

A *more focused* system presupposes the eradication of duplication and overlapping and better coordination. Another requirement is consolidation. At least one area represents top priority – the social and economic sphere.

More efficiency and cost effectiveness implies, as a top priority, the introduction of a management culture, and an increase in productivity through innovation, restructuring and reallocation of resources. Technological changes are the major tool for dealing with these issues. The motto of cost effectiveness today is to do more with less. Of course, reform needs a realistic approach. In this connection I would like to stress that it would be a mistake to consider the UN as an embryo of a world government or an international police headquarters. It is the centre for agreed actions of Member States.

Many suggestions are made in this book to rationalize the work of the *General Assembly*. This is a major feature of the analysis in the book. The General Assembly, at its fiftieth session, discussed about 170 items and approved close to 325 resolutions. There have been proposals to merge or reduce the number of items on its agenda, but the reality is such, that although it is easy to introduce new issues, there is no procedure to easily remove them. Many delegations have suggested limiting the number of periodic reports requested by the Assembly, restructuring the Main Committees and modifying their timetable. Work in the Committees is indeed an extremely time-consuming exercise. It should be noted that many delegates do not limit their participation in the work of the Committee to mere discussion of the texts of resolutions; much time is taken up by long political and, still, even now, ideological statements.

As the UN Under-Secretary-General for Political Affairs, I was heavily involved in the activities of the General Assembly, as well as some of the other UN bodies, and have personally experienced struggling with its drawbacks. Although I do not claim to have the solutions to all of its problems, I do feel, however, that some suggestions presented by the authors deserve special attention. In particular, I believe that a major tool to streamline the decision-making process in the Assembly would be its further regionaliz-ation. In this respect, the European Union provides a good example of regional coordination. Some other groups – for example, the African Group – have also developed mechanisms which harmonize the positions of their Member States. The more work done at the preliminary stage within the groups, the more efficient the functioning of the Assembly. One cannot but recognize that some subsidiary bodies of the General Assembly, for example the Committee on the peace-zone in the Indian Ocean, are already out of date today.

The other major UN organ, the *Security Council*, is currently most often discussed in the press. It bears primary responsibility for the maintenance of peace and security and is the only body that has the power to make decisions obligatory to all Member States, including coercive action. In recent years, the style and the substance of the work of the Council have changed dramatically. There has been considerable growth in its activities, coupled with an unprecedented degree of unity among its members. Recently, the 1,000th resolution was adopted. The veto of the permanent members of the Security Council has nowadays acquired a new meaning. For decades, it played a negative role, blocking the work of the Organization. Today, it plays a different, more positive role as a powerful stimulus for consensus among the permanent five. The other members remain cautious and try not to provoke the permanent members into applying the veto to preserve the existing balance.

A major fact which now provokes the most heated debates is the composition of the Council. It is often considered to be out-dated and not to reflect the realities of the contemporary international political situation. In 1993, the Secretary-General invited Member States to submit their opinions on the restructuring of the Council and received nearly 100 replies from individual States as well as regional groups. Virtually all States favoured an increase in the membership with no voices to the contrary. However, a number of wide-ranging conditions were proposed to help decide on its revised composition. For example, most replies envisaged that the total number of seats in the Council be increased from the current 15 to between 19 and 25, with the number of permanent members growing by at least one and possibly up to seven. Another suggested formula was to include one additional permanent seat per region. It is noteworthy that in this context many Member States accepted the principle of regional arrangements for the rotation of seats. I think this is particularly important. When the veto is not used automatically, the role of the 10 non-permanent members of the Council increases tremendously.

Among other issues of concern to Member States with regard to the Security Council, two attract particular attention. The first is the right of veto. Some countries believe that it is undemocratic and should be at least restricted to certain issues. The other problem is the relationship between the Council and the General

Assembly. A number of delegations have suggested that the Council should be more accountable to the Assembly and that their relationship should, in general, be more balanced and coordinated. This proposal seems to me to be very important in the process of the democratization of the decision-making process within the UN. This matter is dealt with at some length in chapter five.

It is not surprising that the fiftieth session of the General Assembly began with the consideration of the problem of the composition of the Security Council. An Open-Ended Working Group created over a year ago to discuss this issue submitted a report to the Assembly. The substantive findings of the group can be summarized as follows: Important differences continue to exist on key issues before the Open-Ended Working Group, and therefore, further in-depth consideration of these issues is still required. In short, as before, there are as many opinions as there are Member States.

Currently the Council is overwhelmed by the number and complexity of issues under its consideration. Meanwhile, according to the Charter, it can create subsidiary organs and authorize them to consider certain issues. If this concept were to be revitalized, it is possible that the effectiveness of the decision-making process in the Council be considerably improved. However, this has not been done since the 1940s. As pointed out by the authors, perhaps the most vivid example of an unutilized resource is the Military Staff Committee. In theory it was supposed to assist the Council on all questions relating to the use of military force and disarmament and to be 'responsible . . . for the strategic direction of any armed forces placed at the disposal of the Security Council'. In reality it never did any substantive work. Of course, no change in the Charter is needed to render the work of the Security Council more transparent.

While the Security Council stars in many political dramas and is often mentioned in news reports, not much is heard about the *Economic and Social Council*. Initially, ECOSOC was intended to be a similar body to the Security Council in its own sphere of social and economic responsibility. The reform of ECOSOC has been discussed for many years but as yet nothing has been done, as pointed out in chapter seven. Meanwhile an urgent necessity exists to rationalize the subsidiary bodies of ECOSOC. A first step in this direction could be to highlight the role of the Commission on Sustainable Development by, for example, transferring it to Geneva and merging it with the Commission on Science and Technology, Commission on Social Development and Committee on Natural Resources. The necessity also exists to evaluate the structures and mandates of other UN bodies dealing with economic issues, in particular since the creation of the World Trade Organization. The authors make some proposals in these and other areas in chapter eight.

The *Trusteeship Council* is the most vivid example of an under-utilized UN asset. Its initial mandate is now outdated. A proposal has been made to abandon it. However, there remain many actions that this organ could perform for the benefit of the international community. The Maltese proposal in chapter six, to give a new kind of trusteeship to this body – that is, the trusteeship of common heritage – is very interesting. In particular, the Council could be entrusted to provide governance for so-called 'failed States' – countries where government structures have collapsed and where the UN is conducting operations such as those in Cambodia and Somalia.

The authors deal with the question of why reform of the UN is such a slow and painful process. Of course the Members wish to improve the UN. However, there is no consensus among them about ways of achieving this aim and they are not always sure what sort of United Nations they want. For instance, a majority of Member States are encouraging the expansion of UN field activities, assigning new tasks and mandates, with the result that the Organization is becoming involved in spheres where, previously, no international activities existed. In an increasingly interdependent world this is a natural and inevitable process. Often, however, when this occurs a restricted group of Member States will express dissatisfaction and criticism, for example, with UN involvement in the protection of human rights.

There are complaints about the role of the major Powers. It is well known, that the major Powers are also the principal contributors to the UN budget. Of course, the influence of the predominant political actors and large contributors is a fact of life in all international organizations. However, there are only a few such countries, and the other members of the UN are able to have their say, as in any democratic structure, in the new post-cold war world. Within the UN, much depends upon the functioning of the institutions and the degree of activity of a particular country or group of States.

Malta has always played an active role in the UN. Malta's role is referred to in chapter one. Today, in the post-confrontational era, the window of opportunities is widely opened for all countries which are ready to contribute to international politics.

The major problem currently facing the United Nations is the lack of resources. The authors analyse this in chapter nine and make some proposals in this regard. The UN experienced a financial crisis for the first time in the late 1950s, when the Security Council could not agree on the funding of the peace-keeping operations in the Congo and the Middle East. Since then, it has become a chronic illness of the UN, which in recent years has rapidly worsened to become a financial and budgetary crisis. According to UN rules, the annual contributions of Member States should be made by 31 January of each year – but only about 10 per cent of States make their payments on time and some of them are still in arrears for previous years. At the time of writing, the arrears of more than twenty Member States exceed the amount of their two years' contributions. This means that according to the UN Charter they may lose their right to vote.

Nevertheless, despite all its problems and the slow pace of its reform efforts, the United Nations is alive and functioning and able to make a considerable contribution to the strengthening of peace and security. In the last few years it has set up more peace-keeping operations than in its first 40 years. The UN is currently actively involved in the solution of 30 crises and is keeping a close eye on a few dozen other potential zones of conflict. In spite of its importance, peace promotion accounts for only 30 per cent of UN activities. The Organization is involved in all major fields of human endeavour – protection of human rights, economic and social development and protection of the environment, to name but a few. In fact, the UN is already undergoing an adaptation, although to an outside observer this evolutionary process is perhaps not obvious. But, as all living organisms, the UN is constantly growing and developing. Regionalism, the search for a balance of interests and consensus are becoming the driving forces of UN adaptation to the new political environment. I could cite as an example the relations of the UN with OCSE, and the periodic consultations between UN, OSCE,

Council of Europe and ICRC. I deeply believe that the world organization, as a major tool of multilateralism, should in the new emerging international political system, be unequivocally accepted as the framework for any action by States, be it bilateral or unilateral.

There is no alternative to the UN. Only the UN has a universal character – its global convening power and its extensive networks which cover virtually every international function are at the service of all peoples. If, for whatever reason, tomorrow the UN ceased to exist, the international community would have to immediately begin to create a new universal international organization, and whether we like it or not, this new body would be quite similar to the existing UN.

I would like to conclude with a quotation from an ancient philosopher, Seneca. Many centuries ago, he said, 'We were born to live together and our community is like an arch which holds precisely because the stones prevent each other from falling.' I think that this is a very accurate definition of the nature of the United Nations.

Let us redouble our efforts to make the UN, which is needed for all of us, more relevant, more focused and more efficient. I believe that the book of Professor de Marco and Ambassador Bartolo is an important contribution to this end.

CONTENTS

ACRONYMS

ACABQ	Advisory Committee on Administrative and Budgetary Questions
ACC	Administrative Committee on Coordination
APEC	Asia-Pacific Economic Cooperation forum
CCSSD	Commission on Comprehensive Security and Sustainable Development
CPC	Committee on Programme Coordination
CSCE	Commission for Security and Cooperation in Europe (*now* OSCE)
DHA	Department of Humanitarian Affairs
ECA	Economic Commission for Africa
ECE	Economic Commission for Europe
ECLA	Economic Commission for Latin America
ECOSOC	Economic and Social Council
EPTA	Extended Programme of Technical Assistance
ESCAP	Economic and Social Commission for Asia and the Pacific
ESCWA	Economic and Social Commission for Western Asia
EU	European Union
GATT	General Agreement on Tariffs and Trade
IBRD	International Bank for Reconstruction and Development
ICRC	International Committee of the Red Cross
IDA	International Development Association
IMF	International Monetary Fund
NAFTA	North American Free Trade Agreement
NAM	Non-Aligned Movement
NGO	non-governmental organization
ODA	Overseas Development Assistance
OPS	Office of Project Services
OSCE	Organization for Security and Cooperation in Europe
SUNFED	Special United Nations Fund for Economic Development
UNCED	United Nations Conferences on Environment and Development
UNDP	United Nations Development Programme
UNFPA	United Nations Fund for Population Activities
UNHCR	Office of the United Nations High Commissioner for Refugees
UNICEF	United Nations Children's Fund

UNIDO	United Nations Industrial Development Organization
UNV	United Nations Volunteers
WIPO	World Intellectual Property Organization
WTO	World Trade Organization

PREFACE

This second edition of the *Second Generation United Nations*, comes at a time of reflection. Since the publication of the first edition, a number of issues have emerged on the proposed agenda of reform of the Organisation. We have tried to reflect these developments in the new epilogue of this publication listing a number of issues and mechanisms which have been instituted in the field of reform of the United Nations. Indeed ever since the 45th session of the General Assembly, Member States have, in one form or another, been seized with the question of making the United Nations more representative of the needs of the peoples it represents.

Within the broader international context, each event has borne its mark on the Organisation. The end of the Cold War presented us with a reference point. Perhaps what we failed to foresee at the time was that the United Nations was about to embark onto a period of transition wherein it would have to re-orient itself in the face of changing scenarios. Starting with the euphoria which accompanied the concerted international effort to liberate Kuwait, throughout the different crises which we have witnessed on the African continent and most recently with the distress which has been borne by the Kosovo crisis, what has become clear is the fact that the United Nations has embarked into a period of transition.

Historical circumstances have provided this Organisation with unprecedented opportunities for cooperation. Opportunity brings challenges, challenges which we have the responsibility to face and utilise to our advantage.

Many have described the significance of the end of the Cold War. Economic, social and indeed important human and political changes have been the hallmark of the post-cold war era. This has provided a different agenda for the United

Nations. It has also provided a different climate within which the Organisation operates, apparently less confrontational but certainly not less contentious.

More crucially, however, the end of the Cold War provided us with an evolution in the mind-set to which we had been accustomed to for over 50 years. The United Nations was created at a time when the priorities for a stable international order were dictated by the logic of containment. Perhaps the Organisation's greatest ability during those 50 years was indeed its ability to effect a policy within the parameters set by containment policies.

The fall of the Berlin Wall has presented us not only with a different set of priorities and opportunities for action, but has radically changed the basis on which the United Nations rests. Reform for its own sake, reform as an exercise in cost-cutting, reform which merely skirts the periphery, will not yield the required results. We cannot look at the world or the United Nations with the same cold-war lenses. Even less can we seek to reorient the organisation using the same logic.

Yet today we are faced with poignantly challenging questions. The Cold War had provided us with an opportunity to act in concert – in the wake of what we have witnessed with the Kosovo crises, can we truly attest to the ability of the United Nations to represent a truly effective international security structure?

Different crises have engaged the United Nations since the early 1990's. What we witnessed in the wake of the different crises in Africa and other continents, gnawed at our conscience, as we grappled with different tools to deal with the suffering that unfolded there. Yet despite the frustrations and setbacks the United Nations remained engaged. There was, at the minimum, the political will for this international organisation to play its role in accordance with its Charter.

What we have witnessed in the Kosovo case remains markedly different. It has posed challenges to the very *raison d'être* of the Organisation, it has set different parameters in terms of justification for the use of force. It has forced us to set ourselves a number of questions with which we must continue to reckon in the years to come. Ultimately the United Nations will continue to depend on the political will of its members – to act or not to act – the means and measure of the use of force – these are decisions which are dependant on Members of the United Nations.

The most relevant lesson to be learned from all this is, perhaps, the notion of engagement. The United Nations must remain an organisation that engages when situations, clearly within its mandate, arise. To simply act as if the Organisation were not in existence is to the detriment, not only of the organisation itself but to the very notion of a comprehensive international security structure.

Perhaps, within the wider context, the greatest failure of us all has been our inability to transform international relations from a bi-polar (reduced to a mono-polar situation) to a multi-polar system. This remains a crucial task in this time of transition. Bi-polarism led to contained confrontation – multipolarism by its very nature underscores the need for engagement on a co-operative level. In finding ourselves denied this situation, the concern of the void which persists has already unfolded. The United Nations is not to be deemed as the Organisation which is resorted to after events unfold. It has to be the major player in the framing of agreements and the conduct of preventive diplomacy and political settlement.

These remain the challenges for a Second Generation United Nations – one which, conscious of its past, was to embark into the new millennium with a greater commitment to achieve relevance. No amount of efficiency or institutional tinkering will address the fundamentals of a more effective United Nations. This would require a re-thinking of the Organisation in a fundamental manner. To dispute the principles which have guided the United Nations over the past 50 years would upset that delicate balance which inspired the foundation of the Organisation. However to shy away from adapting and applying such principles to the different realities presented today would be shirking our responsibility and that which we owe to future generations.

It is in this spirit that we must view the reform of the United Nations – a reform which requires a sense of comprehensiveness and engagement. We look to the United Nations and seek to establish new parameters: the different committees and different bodies which have been set up as a response to the different periods of history. Some of these retain their usefulness, but require a renewed sense of direction if they are to truly reflect the principles promulgated by the Charter.

At the heart of any reform exercise are the changes which need to be instituted to the principal organs of the United

Nations. The relevance of the General Assembly remains paramount for it is this body which best reflects the notions of universality and democracy. The strengthening of the General Assembly and the instituting of a more symbiotic relationship with the other principal organs of the United Nations is core to our efforts.

This book will illustrate how a number of changes with respect to the agenda of the General Assembly have been instituted. Some limited progress has been achieved. But more needs to be done. This is also true of the Presidency of the General Assembly which rather than reflect a symbolic and procedural role should function on a more political level as representative of the will of the international community. For the President of the General Assembly, not only presides over the Assembly, but represents it and speaks on its behalf.

Such a practice was initiated during the 45th Session of the General Assembly, when the President of the General Assembly* represented its views on a number of issues and initiatives promoting the principles of the Charter. Further changes have been instituted in a piecemeal fashion when dealing with the representation of the President of the General Assembly at meetings of the other principal organs of the Organisation. This is especially the case with the Security Council, although no final agreement on the nature and scope of such involvement has yet been reached. The fact that the President of the General Assembly has since the 45th Session been charged with the chairmanship of the working groups on reform is itself a signal of the acknowledgement that the future of the United Nations lies in the General Assembly.

The President should represent the Assembly in places and situations where the political events so require. He has to represent the Assembly and be the voice of the Assembly in accordance to its resolutions and recommendations. His role, if limited to preside over the Assembly, as to ensure the proper observance of its rules and procedures would amount to reducing the Presidency to a honorific role. This was never the intention of the founding fathers of the United Nations when Paul Henri Spaak was elected as its first President.

---

* Prof. Guido de Marco, one of the co-authors (and now President of Malta) was President of the 45th Session of the General Assembly in 1990-91.

Another proposal which has taken root in recent years is the establishment of the Council of Presidents of the General Assembly which convenes annually to discuss matters relating to the United Nations, its reform and present situation. Such a Council makes recommendations which are then forwarded to the Association of Permanent Representatives for the necessary follow-up. This is another manifestation of the enhanced political role and presence of both the pesonalities but even more of the role of the President of the General Assembly.

There are however other proposals which may further strengthen the General Assembly in areas which have come to affect each and every State. Whether we speak of globalisation in terms of trade or whether we view humanity as being on the brink of a truly living the reality of a global village, one thing is true – what happens on one side of the globe affects each and every one of us. The spread of information technology and media communication ensures that no one is spared from the images of events which occur far beyond national borders.

The nature of the issues themselves have proved to be intrinsically transnational and cannot be confined to the insularity of borders. Whether we speak of the environment, poverty, arms and drugs trafficking – we recognise this basic fact. These phenomena represent effects which go beyond what each part can deal with in isolation. The whole is larger than the sum of its parts – and this is the way we are forced to deal with such issues.

Given such a scenario, the General Assembly moves to the forefront, as the body best suited to foster that international will necessary to combat and confront such issues. But the General Assembly has to change its working habits. To be active from the third week of September to the second week of December and *de facto* hibernate for the rest of the year, does not provide that working structure needed for its role in United Nations affairs.

Keeping the peace has been one of the areas into which the United Nations has ventured into in a most vigorous manner. The continued demands made of the United Nations in regions of conflict and tension have posed both a demand and an opportunity for the General Assembly to play a stronger role. Peacekeeping operations are the result of the engagement by a number of States represented in the General Assembly. The financing of such operations rests also with the general membership. In recognition of this fact the Special Committee on Peacekeeping Operations was established in 1965 with the mandate to undertake a comprehensive review of peacekeeping operations in all their aspects.

This Committee meets annually and discusses generic aspects relating to peacekeeping operations and issues relating to financing of such operations. Alongside this committee regular meetings are held by troop contributing countries on specific aspects of logistics relating to the management of operations in the field.

Much remains to be done on the question of Troop Contributing consultations which is currently being discussed within the Security Council Reform Working Group. However, the impact of decisions and recommendations made by the Special Committee on Peacekeeping spreads over the whole membership of the Organisation and should thus take up a more political role. As a start, its belongingness to the General Assembly makes it well suited to be presided over by the President of the General Assembly, who with his/her further involvement in other meetings and briefings such as those held by the Security Council, is best placed to make an effective contribution to the Committee's work.

Another issue of which the General Assembly has been seized of for a number of years has been the question of Security Council reform. This process has led many to express frustration at the slow pace with which progress unfolds. Rather than view the question of whether the process should be limited to a fixed timeframe, we must recognise the warranted sensitivity surrounding the reform of the Security Council. The majority of States will remain outside the direct purviews of an expansion of the Council and yet continue to raise questions, doubts and legitimate opinions. This should signal the importance which States attach to the Security Council rather than attempts to stall or hamper reform. For a reform to truly be effective it must withstand the test of time. For these reasons, careful deliberation must take place to ensure the best possible Security Council for the United Nations of the new Millennium.

The question of the veto has been repeatedly subjected to discussion and debate. Many have voiced their dissatisfaction with the veto. Others have held that the specific Charter provisions guiding the use of the veto are themselves subject to veto and thus cannot be changed. This state of affairs has often led to polarised debate which rather than help could hinder the true spirit of reform required of the Security Council. Different formulas have been put forward, all seeking to find a common ground based on a notion of *real politik*.

The Security Council requires a studied reform. For the Security Council, as envisaged in the Charter, has what has been described as serious structural limitations in that no action can be taken if one of the permanent members casts its veto, whatever the purpose be, not excluding the use of force by such permanent member.

The Permanent Members of the Security Council remain an anchor in international relations. Apart from commanding a sphere of influence which transcends geographical borders, the mere fact that they have been inscribed as Permanent Members in the Charter of the United Nations is in itself a source of influence which is difficult to negate. Furthermore, the 188 member states of the United Nations have recognised this fact when giving consent to be bound by the Charter.

This, however, does not preclude innovative solutions which may in themselves give an additional weight to the recognition of States with global concerns without necessarily allowing the dilution the general international will. Such a balance could be achieved through a system of weighted voting whereby the Permanent Members of the Council could retain a higher threshold of votes; this system would not give rise to the undermining of the absolute will of the majority. The introduction of quasi permanent members, adequately representing the different regions, can be a positive innovation.

The Charter makes repeated reference to the Military Staff Committee. The Military Staff Committee is there to advise and assist the Security Council on all questions relating to the Security Council's military requirements for the maintenance of international peace and security, the employment and command of forces placed at its disposal, the regulation of armaments and possible disarmament. With the Cold War on, the establishment of the Military Staff Committee consisting of the Chiefs of Staff of the permanent members of the Security Council was a dead letter. Is it still a dead letter?

Ultimately the Security Council must be reinforced as the organ charged with the primary responsibility for the maintenance of international peace and security. Reforms of a realistic nature could, to some extent, ensure the centrality of the Security Council in questions of international peace and security and guard against its marginalisation from major crises as we have witnessed in recent times.

The above are suggestions on how the United Nations, while adhering to the principles which inspired it, may seek to build-in relevance for a changed international climate. The reality with which we are confronted today points to the paramount nature of the political will of the Members of the United Nations. As we have witnessed in recent months, there is no amount of reform which will buttress the role of the United Nations, if this Organisation is simply by-passed in situations which clearly demand its involvement.

We have been attempting to refine and re-define the rules by which the United Nations act. We think we have the tools – we fashion Charters and instruments, we discuss in Committees and in Working Groups – but when such tools fail us, do we not have the responsibility to discuss how to make them work rather than to take a different course of action with unknown parameters? We speak of balance in our approach to security – a balance of human, political and economic factors: does this not mean that the Organisation must work in terms of the Charter, rather than create international police actions by a state or group of states?

There are no hard and fast answers to such questions. What we need to ensure is that the political will exists to play by the rules of the game and not to opt out of the game and move to another one when it does not work - we must be realistic and address the problems with a sense of reality so as to work for changes, so as to make the rules applicable even in a time of transition.

We need the courage to take an honest look at the United Nations Organisation and find ways to effectively address new challenges.

The Trusteeship Council is one such example. This principal organ has had its fate altered by its own success dealing with those former colonial territories in transition. With the attainment of the independence of Palau, the Trusteeship Council's previous mandate has come to a close. Interestingly enough, during the last meeting of the Council, a decision was taken that the Council meet as and when necessary. This is in itself a recognition that the principal organs of the Charter were not merely institutional arms invented for specific tasks but were rather inspired by noble principles deserving of humanity's toil for freedom and prosperity.

PREFACE

It was thus that during the 45ᵗʰ Session, the President of the General Assembly proposed that the Trusteeship Council, which embodied the notion of Trust, be transformed into the guardian of the common heritage of mankind (Chapter 6).

It was in this vein that the President also pointed to the opportunities provided by the Council for those peoples whose economic, political and social structures had broken down. This remains an even more pressing problem that we today face with tragic regularity. The aim of exploring such avenues is not to define, to delimit or to propose borders for sovereignty in terms of territory. This is not the purpose behind the Trusteeship Council nor does it underline our proposal for its reform. The notion of territory is defined more squarely within the purview of the Security Council and the General Assembly.

The notion of Trust has a role to play in ensuring development of peoples, a development which requires both an attention to the environmental conditions prevalent in that which is characterised as the Common Heritage of Mankind, but equally with the social, economic and political development of peoples where such do not, for one reason or another, fall within the purview of a particular State. This is indeed a problem we face with the developments in Kosovo. Perhaps the United Nations may be bold enough to admit that it may hold the solution.

A Second Generation United Nations seeks to outline the paths which reform have taken. It seeks to identify and underline those areas where common ground may be sought. The sensitivity surrounding many of the issues dealt with often hampers us from making creative suggestions to overcome pressing difficulties.

A key aspect of the United Nations in the 21ˢᵗ century will be its relationship with regional arrangements. After the end of the Cold War, in the past decade we have witnessed a rise in incidence of regional conflicts, tension and strife. Regional organisations, in terms of Chapter VIII of the Charter, are well suited to take a leading role in such situations, acting under the aegis of the United Nations.

A United Nations for this new century has to respond to popular expectation and belongingness. We need the expression of a Civil Forum, alongside the workings of a General Assembly which in its composition underlines the inter-governmental aspect of the United Nations. This civil forum can be the expression of the citizens of the world, whether through parliamentary representation both national and regional, or eventually through a directly elected forum. This Civil Forum incorporates also a strong active presence of NGOs covering fields of solidarity and fundamental human rights, and through their emergence influence the United Nations Organisation in a lasting positive effect.

For the United Nations of this century, to remain in the forefront to achieve its objectives, must undergo serious reform. Proposals for reform abound; unless they are followed through by determined political will, they will remain the proposals of academics for academics. Perhaps this time serious consideration will be given to put into effect Article 109 of the Charter:

> "A General Conference of the Members of the United Nations for the purpose of reviewing the present Charter may be held at a date and place to be fixed by a two-thirds vote of the members of the General Assembly and by a vote <u>of any nine members of the Security Council</u>."

This is in itself a recognition made at the time of the drafting of the Charter that inevitable changes would have to be effected if the Organisation was to remain relevant in a changing international context. After fifty-five years, much has happened, the membership of the United Nations has grown from fifty-four to one hundred and eighty-eight, we have witnessed the rise and fall of a Cold War; we have lived the anguish of many a regional conflict; we have seen the demise of empires and ideologies, the birth and resuscitation of states.

The new millennium will continue to present many challenges to the international community. It will also present a number of challenges to the United Nations Organisation which seeks to establish a relevance through its action. We must seize the opportunity to guard against the marginalisation of the United Nations and the principal organs which comprise it. We must seize the opportunity to continue to build relevance into an Organisation which can withstand not only the demands of today but the demands of generations to come.

PREFACE

For the demands will only grow stronger. And only together can we build that stronger Organisation poised to contribute to a better today and towards a better tomorrow.

INTRODUCTION

This study on the United Nations is both a political and structured approach to the working and the future of the Organization. It is not primarily directed at examining the administrative functioning of the UN, but rather at how the United Nations, in a transition process, is managing the future.

We have tried in this study to contribute to the ongoing debate on the revitalization of the United Nations. The United Nations is a very complex system and we do not pretend to have touched upon all its aspects – in part because certain aspects have already been well covered by scholars and experts in international organizations, in part because we preferred to focus on particular areas.

Some of these ideas, initially advanced by Malta at the forty-fifth session of the General Assembly, including the ideas on the Trusteeship Council, have since, in the context of the various high-level working group meetings that have taken place during the 50th Anniversary of the United Nations, also been taken up and promoted by others. We note with satisfaction this indication of their wider acceptance.

Forging changes depends on our ability to identify the signs of our times as much as it relies on our vision of future challenges and discernment of our past. We have been fortunate enough during these last few years to be witnesses and participants to great positive changes.

The breaking down of the Berlin wall may be as decisive to the future of Europe and of global relations as was the storming of the Bastille. Authoritarian regimes in Europe were toppled; the Malta Summit of December 1989 between Bush and Gorbachev, in the words of Edward Shevardnadze, 'buried the cold war'; the Charter of Paris 1990 determined a new concept of democracy and security from Vancouver to Vladivostok. The invasion of Kuwait and the United Nations' determined reaction set the seal to the globalization of change. The world was no longer the same; the bipolar world had ended; new problems were emerging, old problems assumed different dimensions.

What can the role of the United Nations be in this metamorphosis of historical events?

A sense of history may require of us a reassessment of the workings of an evolving United Nations. Political responsibility imposes on us a shared onus to do so.

We identify ourselves with the view that any reforms of the United Nations should be undertaken on the basis of the principle of the sovereign equality of States. We subscribe to the view that the United Nations should deliver its product, in any area of its operations, at the least possible cost. We agree that all marginal activities should be thoroughly reviewed.

In September 1990, Malta was entrusted with the Presidency of the forty-fifth session of the United Nations General Assembly, the first post-cold war session – a session witnessing the gripping concept of democracy extending over the entire Soviet bloc and heralding the break-up of the Soviet Union; a session, however, also scarred by the invasion of Kuwait.

During Malta's presidency of the General Assembly,[1] we were privileged to have an immediate insight into the aspirations of world leaders on the one hand, and the hopes and limits within which the Organization was reacting and adapting to the challenge of change on the other. We called for a Second Generation United Nations, inspiring ourselves by the terminology used in the computer industry rather than the succession of generations of humankind.

We believe that the fundamental principles of the Charter remain as valid as ever. The founding fathers of the United Nations, in charting the future, hitched their wagon to a star. They wanted to assert the equality of all nations large and small; they set as their compass the universal character of human rights; they beckoned for economic development and advancement, making peoples participants thereof. They believed in balance for the maintenance of security through the Security

---

[1] Professor Guido de Marco (one of the authors) presided over the forty-fifth session of the Assembly.

2

Council, having permanent and non-permanent members, the first with veto powers. A 'sixth' veto could be exercised by the non-permanent members if acting in adequate unison.

The evaluation of this balanced approach in the cold war atmosphere was that of a Security Council locked in veto formation and a General Assembly supinely co-existing within the bipolar parameters. There were some events which did effect a world change, even in this atrophied situation: the decolonization process and the birth of new nations large and small.

We intend in this study to work on past experience with a measured audacity as to the future. In particular, we deal with a revitalized General Assembly, as the only organ of the United Nations where all States are permanent members.

We reconsider the concept of the Trusteeship Council revitalizing its future from that of a trusteeship of territories to a trusteeship of the rights of future generations, as the guardian of common concerns, common interests and common heritage of mankind, entrusting the Council with a mandate over the global commons.

We examine the economic structures of the United Nations and their relationship with the Bretton Woods institutions and find them wanting.

We look into the human rights dimension of the United Nations and its linkage not only to individual dignity but also to peace.

We give the notion of peace-keeping our consideration, believing as we do that peace-keeping is an extension of individual State security within an updated concept of regional stability.

Our recommendations and proposals should be received in the spirit in which they are made, namely that they are only proposals for discussion and final decision by Member States. We certainly do not wish to see any activities for the benefit of developing countries, particularly the least developed among them, discontinued, especially if such activities are believed to be useful by such countries.

The reform and revitalization of the United Nations has created world-wide debate. This reflects on and manifests the global interest in the Organization.

We have to be careful, lest in the dialectics of theoretical changes, we fail in the implementation stage, for the United

INTRODUCTION

Nations has proved to be an indispensable forum for dialogue.
It has to prove itself to be an indispensable instrument for world
peace in freedom.

ONE

MALTA'S ROLE IN THE UNITED NATIONS SINCE 1964

Summary

Malta's role in the United Nations was never dictated by its size or by the constraints and limitations of the Organization. A few months after attaining independence in 1964, Malta joined the United Nations which was then in its nineteenth year of existence. Between this time and the next milestone in Malta's participation in the Organization – its presidency of the forty-fifth session of the General Assembly – it made its mark by introducing a number of bold initiatives which became major items on the United Nations Agenda, resulting in General Assembly resolutions and, in some cases, international conventions. Since Malta's General Assembly presidency, certain world events have demonstrated the relevance of some of our ideas and determined that they be pursued with more vigour and urgency. By drawing on our past work and contributions and particularly on the experience of presiding over the work of the General Assembly during its forty-fifth session, we have consolidated our ideas on the restructuring and streamlining of the United Nations and developed them further as a contribution to the debate on the occasion of the Organization's 50th Anniversary.

(a) *Malta and the United Nations*

Malta joined the United Nations in 1964 soon after it gained its independence and thus became the 114th Member State. At that time the United Nations was coming towards the end of its second decade, somewhat more confident than the ill-fated predecessor League of Nations, yet still hesitant in a world dominated by two super-Powers.

Malta's first statement to the world body came amidst an Agenda of the General Assembly that had 83 items (and eight supplementary items)[1] to be covered in the short period of about 10 to 12 weeks, an Agenda that was not too different from the Agenda of the 50th Anniversary of the United Nations. Understandably, the Agenda of the fiftieth session had more items, perhaps many more items than the Assembly could realistically consider. It also had a number of items reflecting the state of the world during 1995–96. But the Agenda of the nineteenth session of the General Assembly, in addition to the items on reports of its subsidiary bodies and agencies, had other items like disarmament (including nuclear disarmament), outer space, the question of Korea, Palestinian refugees, permanent sovereignty over national resources, the question of Cyprus and the question of human rights in, among other places, Algeria, Burundi, China and Cuba.[2]

In such an environment, the then Prime Minister of Malta delivered Malta's first statement to the world body. He presented Malta as a bridge between Africa and Europe and analysed the implications of this matter for Malta and established for Malta its unique role in the Mediterranean. He analysed the work of the United Nations reflected by the various items on the Agenda of the General Assembly and asserted Malta's commitment to the United Nations. Referring to Malta's recently won Independence he committed Malta to the ideals of the United Nations.

On the Agenda of the nineteenth session one also finds references to restructuring and streamlining. This is not surprising since even during the first session of the General Assembly such references had been made. Restructuring and streamlining continues to be a major topic even after the United Nations 50th Anniversary and continues to be a major preoccupation. Henri Spaak, the first President of the General Assembly, in his concluding speech in 1946, said: 'I am not quite sure that the system is entirely good but I must admit that the first attempt which we have witnessed here inspires me with confidence.' It appears that Mr Spaak's doubt sparked more action than did his optimism.

Malta became a member of an Organization which was already

[1] A/57607Rev.2
[2] Ibid.

well established, involved in many areas of human activity and tackling problems that had affected society even before the creation of the United Nations. As seen from the Agenda of the nineteenth session, the United Nations was a reflection of the world at that time. The United Nations is a reflection of the world at any time.

The Headquarters of the United Nations in New York and the main organs of the Organization formed the nucleus of a much larger system consisting of a number of specialized agencies and institutions. This is usually referred to as the United Nations system, as reflected in diagram 1.

It did not take long for Malta to evaluate the work of the Organization and to identify areas which needed improvement and areas where Malta felt it could make a contribution, always keeping in perspective its size and modest resources.

Malta's priorities as can be seen from the development of its Ministry of Foreign Affairs included its work at the United Nations. The Missions to the United Nations in New York and in Geneva were among its earliest representational offices opened.

Malta's work at the United Nations reached a high point during its presidency of the forty-fifth session of the General Assembly in September 1990. Its opening statement affirmed: 'The challenges lying ahead are enormous. But, equally enormous, is the political will to guarantee that mankind's destiny is safeguarded not only by individual countries, but by a strong United Nations. The strength for our actions must be drawn from the tremendous potential which resides in every individual and we must set our objectives in the light of his aspirations for peace and freedom – that freedom which, for every citizen of the world, comes first and foremost.'[3]

(b) *Contributions by Malta*

In the 25 years between its entry into the United Nations and its holding of the Presidency of the General Assembly, Malta had made its mark by participating in the activities of the Organization and by making lasting contributions to its work. Some of the initiatives were:

- 1965, monitoring of the 'dissemination of non-nuclear

[3] UN Doc. A/45/PV.1 (25/09/90), p. 22.

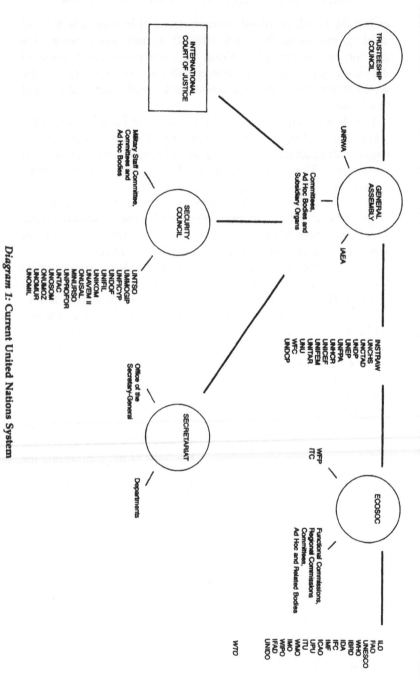

Diagram 1: Current United Nations System

TRUSTEESHIP COUNCIL

INTERNATIONAL COURT OF JUSTICE

GENERAL ASSEMBLY

SECURITY COUNCIL

SECRETARIAT

ECOSOC

UNRWA

IAEA

Committees, Ad Hoc Bodies and Subsidiary Organs

Military Staff Committee, Committees and Ad Hoc Bodies

UNTSO
UNMOGIP
UNFICYP
UNDOF
UNIFIL
UNIKOM
UNAVEM II
ONUSAL
MINURSO
UNPROFOR
UNTAC
UNOSOM
ONUMOZ
UNOMUR
UNOMIL

INSTRAW
UNCHS
UNCTAD
UNEP
UNFPA
UNHCR
UNICEF
UNIFEM
UNITAR
UNU
WFC
UNDCP

WFP
ITC

Office of the Secretary-General

Departments

Functional Commissions, Regional Commissions Committees, Ad Hoc and Related Bodies

ILO
FAO
UNESCO
WHO
IBRD
IDA
IFC
IMF
ICAO
ITU
UPU
WMO
IMO
WIPO
IFAD
UNIDO

WTO

8

weapons', which today has become a reality following the adoption by the forty-eighth session of the General Assembly of resolution 46/36L which established a universal and non-discriminatory register of International Conventional Arms transfers;[4]

- 1966, the general review of the economic and social activities of the United Nations so as to increase substantially aid granted to Member States in the implementation of economic and social programmes of immediate interest to them;[5]

- 1967, application of the concept of the common heritage of mankind to the international seabed and ocean floor, and the subsoil thereof, underlying the high seas beyond the limits of national jurisdiction and agreement that this area would be used for the common benefit of all mankind. This led to the adoption in 1982 of the United Nations Convention on the Law of the Sea (Entry into force on 16th November 1994);[6]

- 1968/69, the problems of the elderly, leading to the convening of the 1982 World Assembly on Ageing and the adoption of the Vienna Plan of Action on Ageing, and the setting up of the International Institute on Ageing in Valletta, Malta with association to the United Nations;[7]

- 1978, the safeguard provision in favour of net importing developing countries in international commodity agreements negotiated under United Nations auspices. This provision was included in the first International Commodity Agreement on Natural Rubber;[8]

- 1983/84, the proposals for strengthening the role of the United Nations Security Council in the containment and prevention of conflicts. This led to the adoption by the Security Council and the endorsement by the General Assembly of a 19-point paper and another follow-up paper on the subject matter. These are today being used

---

[4] UN *Yearbook* 1965, twentieth session of the UN General Assembly, A/C.1/L.347.
[5] This was a 1965 initiative by Prime Minister Dr G. Borg Olivier in his address to the twentieth session of the UN General Assembly.
[6] Res. 2340 (XXII) of 18 December 1967.
[7] ECOSOC res. 1987/41.
[8] Natural Rubber Agreement 1995, article 51, doc. TD/Rubber.3/11.

as a basis for the role of the Security Council in the evolution of a 'new world order';[9]

- 1988, application of the concept of the Common Concern of Mankind to climate change. This led to the adoption of resolution 43/53 on the 'Protection of Global Climate for Present and Future Generations of Mankind' and the preparation of an effective framework convention on this subject (Malta has agreed and ratified the Convention and is one of the original States parties to the Convention);[10]

- 1989, the protection of 'extra-territorial spaces'. Consideration of this item has been taken over by the International Law Commission as part of its agenda on the environmental protection of the 'global commons';[11]

- The strengthening of security and co-operation in the Mediterranean. This led to the adoption by the General Assembly of resolutions by which the International Community has recognized that security in Europe and security in the Mediterranean are inextricably interlinked;[12]

- The special needs of island developing countries leading to the adoption of resolutions that recommended alleviation of the difficulties and handicaps of this group of countries and the construction of an Index of Vulnerability for Island Developing Countries;[13]

- The role of the ocean in climate change, with the aim of assisting Governments in their assessment of the role of the oceans as a source and a sink for greenhouse gases, sea-level rise and climate change, impacts on marine living and non-living resources, and climate change and variability.[14]

---

[9] UN doc. S/15971 of 12 September 1983 and S/16760 of 28 September 1984.
[10] UN General Assembly res. 43/53 of 6 December 1988.
[11] UN General Assembly forty-fourth session.
[12] UN General Assembly resolutions (latest res. 49/81 of 15 December 1994).
[13] Various UN General Assembly resolutions including res. 49/100 of 19 December 1994 and also the Report of the Global Conference on the Sustainable Development of Small Island Developing States held in Barbados in 1994 (doc. A/Conf./167/9).
[14] Sixteenth session of the IOC Assembly, March 1991.

(c) *Malta and the Presidency of the General Assembly*

Malta assumed the presidency of the General Assembly at a time of unprecedented developments in the world – the summit meeting between President George Bush and President Mikhail Gorbachev in Malta, less than a year before, signalled the end of the cold war and the end of the division of Europe which had begun at Yalta.

On the other hand the Organization was being tested with the way it was going to deal with the Gulf Crisis following Iraq's invasion of Kuwait. This was a time when the shortcomings of the Organization had to be laid bare while at the same time it could not afford to let aggression go unchallenged.

We saw this opportunity to preside over the General Assembly as an occasion to draw on past experience in the work of the Organization and as a chance to be perhaps a little bolder than previous holders in reflecting developments that were taking place in the world around us. It is in the same spirit that we launch this study. By drawing on our past work at the United Nations and particularly on the year that the presidency of the General Assembly was held by Malta we wish to contribute to the 50th Anniversary of the Organization with our proposals for a Second Generation United Nations. We consider fifty years to be sufficient to enable us to evaluate the successes and failures of the Organization. The 50th Anniversary should be an opportunity to rededicate ourselves to the Charter which we still believe to be the best guarantee for peace in freedom in the twenty-first century.

The concluding statement to the forty-fifth session of the General Assembly recalled that Henri Spaak, the first President of the General Assembly, had observed that the United Nations was more of a meeting of statesmen than a meeting of diplomats. This raised the expectations of the first President and he hoped that this might have been the 'missing element' in the ill-fated League of Nations. Expectations are one thing, however, and reality another! In our opinion, the United Nations continues to be predominantly a 'meeting' of diplomats with only marginal involvement of statesmen. This may be the basic flaw of the United Nations today and unless the 'missing element' is introduced no change, restructuring or streamlining is going to help. It is for this reason that we propose to introduce this 'missing element' in the form of a political structure, which could take various forms, to give the United Nations the political authority that is so far lacking. In the same statement it was emphasized that the United Nations has first to be made relevant before it is made efficient, because the pursuit of efficiency without relevance would be a step backwards.

(d) *Revitalization and Restructuring of the United Nations*

Work on the revitalization and restructuring of the United Nations has proliferated from the earliest days of the Organization. There is certainly no lack of proposals and recommendations. In fact, some of our own proposals may have already been included or repeated in some of the other studies. The 50th Anniversary of the United Nations has encouraged another wave of such reviews and studies. Some of them have been initiated from within the United Nations – others from outside.

We are sure that all such efforts can only enrich the debate and are an indication of the concern that everyone has for the United Nations to be as effective as possible to guarantee peace and freedom in the world. Some questions that come to mind immediately are: with this wealth of proposals and recommendations – with more still to come – why have no significant proposals and recommendations been implemented yet? What is wrong with the *Agenda for Peace* or the *Agenda for Development*?

In attempting to answer these questions one has to be guided by a sense of realism. In the words of the previous Secretary-General Pérez de Cuéllar: 'The United Nations is not a super-State. It is an organization of independent and sovereign nations: it has no sovereignty of its own.' In other words, the United Nations can only be as efficient and as effective as its Member States would like it to be. It has been obvious so far that a consensus on this matter has not yet been reached. The difference between the rhetoric and the practice in this regard has been and remains staggering. We should not underestimate the magnitude of the problem of reaching a consensus among the 185 Member States on such important matters as the expansion of the Security Council and the use of force in accordance with articles 43 and 45 of the Charter. In the circumstances, we have no doubt that the only proposals and recommendations that will be eventually implemented will be those that enjoy the support of all the Member States. It is for this reason that, in our own discussions, ideas, and proposals, we have kept this sobering thought in mind. It is for this reason that we have endeavoured to be realistic and pragmatic whenever we were tempted to consider some utopian alternatives. We feel that our views in this regard are practical and can be accepted by all.

No remedy, no matter how effective and no matter how desirable, can cure a malady or an illness unless it is administered. Recommendations, proposals and ideas for a better United Nations would be useless unless they are implemented. There are so many ideas which deserve to be adopted that it would be a great pity if they were ignored.

On the other hand such ideas are so numerous that it would be impossible for the General Assembly to take action on a number of them without some further work. We think that everyone would agree that the time has come to move from proposing new ideas to actually implementing some of them.

It would be fitting we think to agree that the fifty-first session be designated as the 'enabling' or 'implementing' Assembly and 1997 as the Year of the Second Generation United Nations. The fifty-first session of the General Assembly should approve a series of recommendations and proposals that will launch the Second Generation United Nations.

TWO

FROM THE
LEAGUE OF NATIONS TO
THE UNITED NATIONS

Summary

That the United Nations has lasted 50 years is in itself an accomplishment. A third world war could have been the culmination of the cold war era – although what role the United Nations played in this regard is not certain. That the end of the cold war made the United Nations less important is certainly not true. The unexpected proliferation of regional conflicts, if anything, made the United Nations more, not less important. Yet, the United Nations' experience shows that the institution has not risen to this challenge and thus did not meet the increased expectations of the international community. This continues to intrigue and concern Member States. The 50th Anniversary of the Organization should be used as an opportunity to identify the reasons for this shortcoming and to propose ways in which it can be overcome. The brief historical analysis of the transition from the League of Nations to the United Nations in this chapter will serve as background for the development of what in our opinion are the reasons why the United Nations, in spite of some successes, continues to be perceived as ineffective and unable to meet the expectations of its Members.

(a) *The League of Nations (1920–1939):*
the Failure and its Causes

'Mankind is once more on the move'

The League of Nations was established in 1920, following the First World War, as a medium to control further international

14

crises. It was the first effort in world history to create an international organization, with a permanent body, to oversee relations between the States of the world. Jan Christian Smuts expressed the spirit accurately when writing that 'Mankind is once more on the move.'[1]

The League was organized around an Assembly (54 Members and 6 Commissions) as well as a Council (5 permanent members and 5 non-permanent members in 1930), each body requiring a unanimous vote of those present for a decision to be binding. The Covenant also provided for a Secretariat and a myriad of intergovernmental or expert committees. The League's interests were diverse, ranging from disarmament, intellectual cooperation, mandates, economic and financial issues. Most of these matters of concern were later broken up between the early specialized agencies of the United Nations. The number of civil servants of the League totalled 670 while the total budget during the years of principal activity varied between 2.5 and 7 million US dollars annually,[2] relatively substantial figures. In fact, limiting the budget and cutting down expenses of the League were constant preoccupations throughout the life of the organization.

The Covenant of the League of Nations was a treaty incorporated in several other Peace Treaties, including the Versailles Treaty. The Covenant moulded the indivisible peace idea: if one State is insecure, all States are insecure. In principle, a threat to peace in any part of the world had to lead to a collective response by the Members of the League. Although the League's Treaty enshrined the notion of collective security in Articles 10, 11 and 16, it provided only vague obligations to ensure its functioning, especially with respect to the States suffering from an attack violating the provisions of the Covenant. Furthermore, any decision taken by either the Assembly or the Council had to be the result of a unanimous vote, often an obstacle to any intervention to preserve international peace.

Unfortunately, enthusiasm for the League was to fade away in less than a decade, following a series of failures to maintain the peace. Collective security went bankrupt from the 1930s on,

---

[1] Cited in Scott, George *The Rise and Fall of the League of Nations*, London, Hutchinson & Co Ltd, 1973; p. 30.
[2] LeRoy Bennett, A., *International Organizations: Principles and Issues*, Fifth Edition, New Jersey, Prentice Hall Inc, 1991; p. 32.

as evident in the League's handling of the cases involving the great Powers of the time. To name only a few: the Japanese occupation of Manchuria (1931), the Italo-Abyssinian conflict (1935–36) and, as a culminating point, the Second World War. In the Manchurian conflict, the great Powers reacted weakly, showing more support to Japan than to China. In addition, once the Assembly examined the issue in order to find a settlement, Japan withdrew from the League. The unwillingness to recognize Manchurian China's interests led to a collective delegitimization and, by the same token, announced that the Second World War was imminent. As for the Italo-Abyssinian case, it was a considerable failure for the League of Nations. Although the Council declared that Italy's intervention was illicit and sanctions should follow, no Member State complied with the embargo. Clearly, all these cases demonstrated that there was no feeling of international responsibility on the part of the sovereign Member States.

The deficiency of the collective security system is the result of various factors. As seen previously, the main problem of the League was that collective security failed when it addressed disputes involving the great Powers. Neither Great Britain nor France felt it was their duty to act in order to secure international peace. The major Powers did not seem to bear responsibilities for the working of the international system. In the end, the Member States proved unable to enlarge their view of national interest to risk the lives of their own soldiers in conflicts in which they were not directly involved. Moreover, the Covenant did not make war illicit. The peaceful settlement of disputes was not mandatory, only the attempt to settle disputes was. Article 12 stated that after a three-month period, if the conflict remained unsolved, the parties could resort to war. Thus, the maintenance of peace was not based on war avoidance. This may have in fact been the most basic flaw of the League.

The League's problems were further enhanced by its limited membership both in terms of number as well as power. Indeed, the United States was not a Member, while the powerful States that were Members did not oppose aggressor countries when it had been necessary. Thus, the membership structure was corollary to the lack of concerted action.[3] In addition, under

[3] *Ibid.*, p. 38.

Article 1, any Member could withdraw from the League, thereby reducing the legitimacy of the League as an *international* institution. Germany and Japan, withdrawing in 1933 and by the same token triggering a series of defections, espoused the built-in weakness of the League with respect to its membership dispositions. Unfortunately, the membership question was not completely solved through the creation of the United Nations: membership of bodies such as the Disarmament and Human Rights Committees is still confined to a limited number of participants. The United Nations, as the League of Nations, still incorporates a tension between decision-making based on unanimity and on a concert formula (agreement among major Powers).

The area in which the League performed most successfully was in the economic and social realm, as the Covenant provided for fair labour conditions, supervision of drug traffic and arms trade as well as concern for disease control.[4] The United Nations learned from this and embodied the above issues in the new Charter so that international cooperation and development became tools to secure a peaceful international system.[5] In fact, one may say that the United Nations was less successful in this area than the League itself. The United Nations, it seems, learned more from the failures than from the limited successes of the League of Nations. Still, one may wonder: did the United Nations learn enough?

(b) *The United Nations: Lessons from the Past*

The first session of the General Assembly of the United Nations had not even concluded, and Member States were already establishing groups and committees to improve the performance of the Organization as if to allay the concerns of the General Assembly's eminent first President. Perhaps the collapse of the League of Nations was too fresh in the minds of the founder Members of the United Nations so that they wanted to avoid the same fate for the newly found Organization. Whether the phenomenon of United Nations restructuring, which was launched more or less with the United Nations itself, made the Organization more

[4] Covenant of the League of Nations, Article 23.
[5] Waters, Maurice, *The United Nations*, New York, The MacMillan Company, 1967; p. 9.

effective and efficient, is questionable. The continued preoccupation with restructuring the Organization is the most significant evidence that the structure has failed to meet its ambitious goals.

During the spring of 1945, after almost a year of discussion on the establishment of a new international organization, a final Charter for the United Nations Organization was inaugurated. The Organization was to be a new vehicle for peace, yet it maintained several attributes of the late League of Nations. In effect, the League and the United Nations shared to a great extent the objectives, the method and the structure to achieve peace and security.[6]

The main bodies of the League, such as the Assembly and the Council, were recycled in the United Nations' system. The General Assembly differed from the League's Assembly in that it acquired more power, mostly as a result of small States' pressure. The expansion of authority was apparent particularly in the social and economic fields which were previously under the responsibility of the Council of the League. Similarly to the Council of the League, the Security Council of the United Nations was given much power through the veto capacity of its permanent members,[7] its responsibility for security matters and its authority to use regional organizations in order to enforce peace. The Secretary-General also acquired more power under the Charter of the United Nations than the Secretary-General of the League. Particularly with respect to his increased political role, provided by Article 99 which allows the Secretary-General to 'bring to the attention of the Security Council any matter which in his opinion may threaten the maintenance of international peace and security'.

In addition to structural lessons, the fatalistic experience of the League inspired the founding fathers of the United Nations to learn from the functional flaws of the League. One of them was that collective security had failed because the Covenant did not include an explicit obligation for the Member States to participate in the repression of an act of aggression. Moreover, the League could not exercise any credible threat since there was no armed

---

[6] *Ibid.*, p. 24.
[7] It is worth noting that States such as Uruguay believed the voting formula entrenching a veto for the major Powers was a transitional arrangement (Waters, *op. cit.*, p. 11).

body acting in its name.[8] To reinforce collective security, the United Nations Charter designated the great Powers, members of the Security Council, as responsible for peace maintenance. Nonetheless, all members would have to contribute armed forces upon the Security Council's demand. The Charter also provided for a Military Staff Committee to advise the Council on security matters. The rationale for granting such a high degree of power to the Security Council was to confer to the major Powers a clear responsibility for the maintenance of international peace. Concentrating security obligations in a concerted manner was considered to be a step to increase the sense of *collective security* rather than *self-help* as it had characterized the League. This was seen as a crucial factor, maybe explaining why no sanction was applied to Italy during its conflict with Abyssinia. One may also conjecture whether, if Great Britain or France had intervened through the League of Nations, Japan might have been restrained and the Second World War might not have taken shape the way it did. In contrast, during the Gulf War, Chapter VII on breaches to the peace and acts of aggression was applied word for word with respect to sanctions imposed on Iraq.

A related lesson the United Nations learned from the League's experience was to prohibit the use of force unless used in the name of collective action or self defence.[9] The League's Covenant legitimized war if peaceful settlement failed; the Charter, however, made the international use of force illicit except in two specific cases: self-defence and following a decision of the Security Council. The difference between both institutions may be phrased as the League of Nations *maintaining order*, while the United Nations role is to *maintain peace.*

The rule of unanimity had also been a problem facing the League that would be tackled by the new Organization. The United Nations Charter states that the General Assembly's decisions are reached by majority vote and that in the case of important decisions, a two-thirds majority is required. For the Security Council, should no permanent member apply its veto, nine affirmative votes out of fifteen are required.

Another lesson understood from the League's experience was that it had been too restrictive. In contrast, the United Nations came to incorporate the United States as well as all the newly

[8] Bertrand, Maurice, *L'ONU*, Paris, Editions La Découverte, 1994; p. 22.
[9] Charter of the United Nations, Article 51.

independent countries, which gave more credibility to the Organization as a body representing the world community.

Nonetheless, the League's major flaw remained the lack of political will on the part of its Members. Hence the first goal of the United Nations founding fathers was to secure a willingness to act, and this was embodied in Article 2 of the Charter which emphasizes the Member's responsibility to fulfil the obligations arising from the Charter and to assist the United Nations in any operation. In our view, in spite of the legal embodiment of Member States' responsibility, the lack of political will continues to be a major consideration in the work and significance of the United Nations. A new restructured United Nations would need to overcome this flaw.

(c) *The United Nations: Lessons from the Present and for the Future*

We have witnessed alarming changes in the world over the last few years. Too often, however, the United Nations has not responded successfully to these challenges. Some crises, for instance, might have been averted – *before* they became too destructive – by a United Nations that was able and willing to exercise fully the kinds of powers envisaged in the Charter. Moreover, all the related agencies would have worked together to support these United Nations goals. What would an ideal United Nations have done in some of these recent crises and what lessons may we draw for the future?

The Gulf War brought out an institutional weakness that also characterized the League of Nations. Many had argued that the League of Nations was mostly a victors' club since small and neutral Powers did not gain much representation during the drafting of the League's Covenant and afterwards.[10] The same criticism directed at the United Nations system had been articulated by the Non-Aligned Movement. Some questioned whether, had Iraq been involved in the Security Council's discussion concerning intervention in the Gulf region, it would have been more likely that the international community could have reached a peaceful diplomatic solution. In addition, the involvement of world opinion through the United Nations forum might have

---

[10] Scott, *op. cit.*, p. 15.

had a positive influence and persuaded Iraq to move out of Kuwait.

Peace can never be secured without the promise of development. In the case of Somalia, one may wonder whether the poverty and famine that afflicted its people could have been addressed earlier and effectively by United Nations economic and social agencies. In particular, could development agencies such as the World Bank, assisted by the UN in its trusteeship role, by attacking the roots of the problems have ensured that the inhumane suffering related to the famine and poverty would never have occurred? Once civil war breaks out and the political and social structure of the society is destroyed, one can study the possibility of having that State and its people placed under the trusteeship of the United Nations, which, in safeguarding sovereignty, could then intervene to provide the basic services necessary. For this and other reasons, we propose a new role for the Trusteeship Council.[11] The early intervention of the Second Generation Trusteeship Council may contribute to limit the tragedy in States whose social and political structures are under stress.

In Rwanda, much like Somalia, poverty and ethnic tensions formed a dangerous mix. A Second Generation United Nations, in particular through an effective ECOSOC and a Trusteeship Council with a new role, might have been able to defuse the foundations of the problems by addressing the economic and social deficiencies of the country. Again, development agencies, such as the World Bank, could have been more deeply involved in helping to alleviate the crippling poverty. An effective United Nations could have contributed to limiting the ethnic tensions before they exploded into violence by mediating between parties or helping to impose and enforce a just peace and democracy, if necessary through a trusteeship arrangement.

Haiti also presented a challenge that mixed extreme poverty and a lack of democracy. Here, the United Nations system could have been energized to guide the Haitian people towards a more democratic and prosperous path. The United Nations' second attempt at this seemed to have worked. A close analogy can be drawn with the United Nations role in Namibia where it helped

[11] See chapter six of this work.

that country's transition towards democracy and an effective domestic government.

These examples show clearly the difference between an ideal United Nations and the organization that is actually functioning today. What lessons should be drawn from the examples above and what kind of guidelines may be extracted for the future? First, the United Nations should address problems *before* they become problems. Preventive diplomacy needs to be strengthened and the United Nations empowered to act quickly and forcefully to stop crises from escalating. Secondly, international peace and development must be seen as part of the same holistic process. The economic and social integrity of all people, but particularly the eradication of poverty, must be addressed in order to guarantee peace, freedom and advancement. Thirdly, the United Nations, or any relevant regional organization, should assist directly in domestic affairs when the basic domestic institutions seem to be breaking down. It should be the aim of United Nations interventions to work through collective security to restore the capacity of countries to govern and provide for their own people, thereby ensuring peace to the international community. Fourthly, these examples show how important mobilizing political will is to ensuring a successful United Nations. Successes in the past, such as the fight against apartheid and the process of decolonization, demonstrate clearly how much can be accomplished, while situations like ex-Yugoslavia and Rwanda demonstrate that failure is inevitable when this political will is absent.

It is in this context that the institutional requirements of the United Nations should be viewed. It is in this context that we see the roles of a rejuvenated ECOSOC, a refocused Trusteeship Council and a revitalized General Assembly to increase the relevance of the Charter as it relates to the betterment of humankind.

THREE

SURVEY OF PREVIOUS STUDIES, STRATEGIES AND REPORTS ON THE RESTRUCTURING OF THE UNITED NATIONS

Summary

Studies, strategies and reports on how to improve the United Nations have proliferated in recent years. The strategies, the *Agenda for Peace* and the *Agenda for Development* as well as other proposals from within the system, like the New Dimensions of Arms Regulation and Disarmament in the post-cold war era, have been supplemented by other comprehensive studies from outside. In this chapter we analyse some of these and endeavour to see why in spite of so rich a harvest of proposals and recommendations, so little was done to change the United Nations. This chapter gives only a sample of the most recent reform proposals. These and other studies and recommendations which, we believe, also deserve attention and consideration, are summarized in annexe I.

(a) *A Decade of Studies and Reports*

On the occasion of the 40th Anniversary of the United Nations, Maurice Bertrand prepared a report for the Joint Inspection Unit, a United Nations body, on reforming the Organization. This report, entitled *Some Reflections on Reform of the United Nations*, became known as it came out in the context of a UN crisis, when there was widespread acknowledgement that the Organization did not live up to Members' expectations.

What Maurice Bertrand suggested in this report was a change of the United Nations Organization from a mainly political body to a broader political and economic institution. To shape this 'economic United Nations', Bertrand recommended a total restructuring of the development organs of the UN in order to transfer them to the regional level. In addition, in his view, reforms should be geared towards the creation of a world forum, an Economic Security Council (ESC), dealing solely with economic issues. This Council would replace ECOSOC and UNCTAD. As for its membership, the Council would include developing countries, with at most 23 members – enough to represent the major Powers and regions of the world system.[1] Other reforms suggested by Bertrand included the creation of a centralized interdisciplinary secretariat and smaller secretariats within each specialized agency; the replacement of the Administrative Committee on Co-ordination (ACC) by councils and commissions; and the involvement of high-level officials in each delegation, one for economic affairs and the other for political matters.

To realize this, Maurice Bertrand delineated three necessary steps: preparing a detailed blueprint for a reformed UN, implementing without delay preliminary reforms, and designing a transition plan. The transition plan was to include how the resources would be transferred to the regional development agencies and how the various UN secretariats and larger agencies would be reorganized to concentrate economic services under one division rather than being fragmented into the various agencies of the United Nations.

A second set of proposals came from Marc Nerfin, whose main contribution to the literature on reforming the United Nations was the concept of representation for the people of the world. This idea does not differ too much from a proposal made by the Commission on Global Governance referred to later. His most notable suggestion remained the establishment of a three-chamber United Nations in which the decision-making power would be shared between the *Prince* (governments), the *Merchant* (economic powers) and the *Citizen* (civil society). In this model, a reformed UN system would preserve States' authority through the Prince Chamber, while the Merchant Chamber would incorporate multinational corporations as well as other economic

---

[1] Bertrand, Maurice, *Some Reflections on Reform of the United Nations*, JIU/REP/ 85/9, Geneva, 1985, p. 62.

24

players. Finally, the Citizen Chamber would represent international social actors, be they the people or their associations.

Nerfin's concern in bringing more democracy to the United Nations seemed relevant, yet his project had certain flaws. For example, he did not define the potential powers to be held by the three Chambers, nor did he clarify the make-up of the tripartite relationship. Would the Prince Chamber rule over the other Chambers or would the Citizen's Assembly be given the most power? Moreover, was a reform of the UN Charter linked with the reforms he suggested? These questions were left unanswered. Equally, Nerfin did not expand on the process leading to a three-tier United Nations.

Another reform effort, the Nordic UN Project, was launched in 1989 by four Nordic countries: Denmark, Finland, Norway and Sweden. The Project took shape over three years before the final report was completed.

The Project addressed the UN's deficiencies with respect to its activities in the economic and social fields. The proposals outlined in this study aimed at reforming the management structure as well as the system in place for financing development operations. As it condemned the fragmentation of the UN's development activities, the Nordic Project suggested the establishment of an *International Development Council* (IDC) in order to guide and coordinate the Organization's development activities. In addition, the Project called for the creation of smaller governing bodies, based on universality and representative membership, which would increase the efficiency of development agencies such as UNDP and UNICEF (the Governing Council of UNDP was recently replaced by a smaller Executive Board).

Finally, the Project suggested a three-tier alternative to voluntary funding, including assessed contributions from all Member States, negotiated pledges and voluntary contributions. This appeared to be an interesting formula promoting a more democratic profile of the UN's economic and social organs.

(b) *An Agenda for Peace and an Agenda for Development*

In June 1992 the Secretary-General of the United Nations presented a 50-page report entitled *An Agenda for Peace* covering the Organization's role in promoting and maintaining world peace and security in the 1990s and beyond. The report focused mainly on international security issues and the means to improve preventive diplomacy, peace-keeping, peace-making and peace-building through the United Nations Organization.

Most propositions of the *Agenda* were based on a return to the security system as it was initially envisaged in the United Nations Charter. This included a Security Council checking aggressors with military and economic sanctions, contribution of armed forces by the Member States, and the creation of a Military Staff Committee. As a supplement to the provisions set out in the Charter, Peace-enforcement Units would be created. These units would consist of ready-made contingents available according to the needs of the Security Council. Again, this addition would not have presupposed a radical reform of the security mechanisms entrenched in the Charter since 'such peace-enforcement units [would] be warranted as a provisional measure under Article 40 of the Charter'.[2] Moreover, to further promote peace-making, it was argued that the General Assembly should have increased powers to call for an intervention and that the ICJ role should be reinforced.

The Agenda also emphasized the need for efficient preventive diplomacy through increasing fact-finding missions, an early-warning system and assisting States in order to promote a peaceful settlement of disputes. As for peace-keeping itself, the Agenda called for a clarification of Member States' military contribution to the Organization; providing further training in peace-keeping; improving the capacity of the military staff within the Secretariat; and creating a stock of peace-keeping equipment. On a more general level, social and economic cooperation between Member States as well as cooperation between United Nations and regional bodies was seen as a solution to promote security. To pursue these reforms, the Agenda suggested the creation of a revolving peace-keeping reserve fund, and the immediate appropriation by the General Assembly of one-third of the estimated costs of any new peace-keeping operation decided by the Security Council.

The *Agenda* itself did not envisage many structural reforms, but merely called for reinforcing the existing organs. For example, it encouraged greater consensus for the Security Council and the

[2] Boutros-Ghali, Boutros, *An Agenda for Peace*, United Nations, New York, 1992, p. 26.

continued involvement of the Foreign Ministers in the Council.[3] In addition, it is questionable to what extent visionary principles for peace and security could really lead to concrete reforms. For example, concerning democracy within the Organization, the *Agenda* stated that 'all organs of the United Nations must be accorded, and play, their full and proper role so that the trust of all nations and peoples will be retained and deserved'.[4] The call for 'a strong, efficient and independent international civil service whose integrity is beyond question' was not matched by a blueprint for reforming the current civil service.

In response to the *Agenda for Peace*, Gareth Evans, then Australian Minister of Foreign Affairs, published a comprehensive global agenda for the 1990s and beyond entitled *Cooperating for Peace*.

Some of his recommendations were valuable, particularly in the areas of peace-making and peace-keeping. For example, improving the Secretariat organization and planning, creating a stock of military equipment, increasing the capacity of small planning groups within the Department of Peace Operations, establishing a General Staff in charge of planning and managing the peace-keeping operations, financing peace-keeping operations directly from the United Nations budget, creating a unified budget for peace-keeping and using military alliances to allow a rapid deployment of forces. On the more general question of financing, a tax on international air travel was suggested as well as deprivation of voting rights when a State is in arrears.

Evans also suggested the creation of Peace and Security Resource Centres to carry out preventive diplomacy and dispute resolution. Furthermore, to improve the Organization's preventive diplomacy, it was suggested to improve information flows identifying threats to peace, to set up additional training in dispute resolution, and to use regional organizations and create preventive diplomacy teams.

On restructuring the Secretariat, Evans suggested the appointment of four Deputy Secretary-Generals in order to free the Secretary-General, and thus allow him to focus on priority tasks. Each Deputy Secretary-General would be responsible for a different area: peace and security, economic and social,

[3] *Ibid.*, pp. 45–6.
[4] *Ibid.*, p. 47.

humanitarian, and administration and management.[5] The sections acting under each Deputy Secretary-General would amalgamate the numerous existing organs responsible for either security, economic and social, humanitarian or administrative functions.

In addition, Evans discussed reforms of the Security Council. In his view, the rise of new economic Powers since the UN's creation has suggested that membership of the Security Council should be expanded. However, should there be an enlargement of the Council, Evans opposed any extension of the veto power beyond the status quo. We share this view.

Although the idea of restructuring the system from the existing organs seemed appropriate, we feel that he did not give sufficient consideration to the General Assembly and to other organs such as the Trusteeship Council.

The *Agenda for Peace* was followed two years later by *An Agenda for Development*. Both studies, contributions of the Secretary-General, were meaningful since all Member States had had an opportunity to make comments and contributions to these basic documents. Nevertheless, moving from broad principles to concrete reforms may be problematic.

The *Agenda for Development* was further articulated in collaboration between ECOSOC and a Group of Experts convened by the President of the forty-eighth session of the General Assembly. The discussions centred around the linkage between development, peace and security, the challenges of prioritizing people's involvement in growth and development, as well as the impact of globalization in an increasingly interdependent world, particularly with respect to communications and capital flows.

The *Agenda for Development* acknowledged the logical link between world peace and development. Indeed, there can be no peace without development since 'the lack of development contributes to international tension and to a perceived need for military power.'[6] To achieve sustainable economic development, the report called for governments to make development issues as much a priority as security concerns. The report also emphasized the need for social development: 'people must participate

---

[5] It is to be noted that these suggestions were similar to those in Childers and Urquhart, *Towards a More Effective United Nations*, Development Dialogue 1991: 1–2, Dag Hammarskjöld Foundation, Uppsala, Sweden.

[6] *Agenda for Development*, A/48/935, 6 May 1994, p. 6.

actively in formulating their own goals, and their voice must be heard in decision-making bodies as they seek to pursue their own most appropriate path to development.'[7]

To realize any of the ideas presented in the *Agenda*, the Secretary-General suggested a return to the role assigned in the Charter to development organs, these functions not being entirely fulfilled up to now. As will be seen later, this is our view as well. The link between the *Agenda for Peace* and the *Agenda for Development* was in this case obvious.

Most of the recommendations concerned the need for greater policy coherence and coordination among the development organs of the United Nations, such as UNDP and the Bretton Woods institutions. This was to be achieved through an emphasis on the 'country strategy' of the UNDP and also through the strengthening of the Resident Coordinator system. Moreover, a revitalization of ECOSOC was seen as one remedy against overlaps in the United Nations organs involved in development activities. In the end, the *Agenda* has to be seen as a 'search for a revitalized vision of development' and therefore its purpose is to 'offer guidelines for thought and action by each Member State'.[8]

(c) *More Recent Studies*

Another source of reform proposals came from Erskine Childers and Brian Urquhart who have written extensively on the topic of UN reforms. *Renewing the UN System* was their 1994 attempt to paint the panorama of a New United Nations.

Childers and Urquhart's proposals for new organs included the establishment of a UN System Consultative Board responsible for ensuring that the UN is effective and cohesive; the transformation of the Trusteeship Council into a UN Council on Diversity, Representation and Governance dealing with ethnic minority issues; the establishment of a UN Humanitarian Security Police ensuring safe transport and supply as well as general protection of UN and NGO emergency staff; the creation of a UN Parliamentary Assembly, representing the people; the replacement of ACC with an Executive Committee of the UN system; and the appoint-

---

[7] *Ibid.*, p. 20.
[8] *Ibid.*, p. 42.

ment of an 'ombuds-panel' reviewing the Organization's activities with respect to human rights.

Concerning the General Assembly, Childers and Urquhart called for the creation of a single UN Development Authority encompassing all the existing dispersed development resources, implementing annual theme meetings for ECOSOC and a question period. In addition, it was suggested that all development assistance be concentrated into one United Nations office based in any developing country, this in light of a general trend towards decentralizing the Organization's activities to the regional level.

As a reform of the Secretariat, the appointment of four Deputy Secretary-Generals was suggested, each concentrating respectively on international economic cooperation and sustainable development, humanitarian affairs, political security and peace affairs, and administration and management. A Documentation Unit would also be created to support the Secretariat. The Bretton Woods institutions were also to be restructured into three *equitable* specialized agencies.

Most of the above suggestions were to be achieved without a radical restructuring of the United Nations system, nonetheless several proposals, such as the UN Parliamentary Assembly, still required amendment of the Charter.

In another reform effort, the Commission on Global Governance was established in 1992 as a result of the Stockholm Initiative on Global Security and Governance. Its mandate was to assess the means necessary to improve global security and governance.

In *Our Global Neighbourhood*, the Commission proposed setting up new organs such as Consultative Committees for each peacekeeping operation, a Council of Petitions involving non-State actors and focusing on security matters, and a UN Volunteer Force to deal with first-stage crises and, by the same token, back up preventive diplomacy by reinforcing any threat of UN intervention.

While ECOSOC would be discontinued, as well as UNCTAD and UNIDO, the Commission called for financial and economic reforms. These included establishing a distinct body, the Economic Security Council (ESC), that would pilot economic, social and environment-related activities; weighted voting in the Bretton Woods institutions according to a purchasing power parity GDP; expanded IMF low-conditionality compensatory finance and a renewed issue of SDRs; and a global taxation scheme.

The Commission also put forward the creation of Civil Society Organizations accredited to the General Assembly, as well as a Senior Adviser on Women's Issues in the Office of the Secretary-General and in the specialized agencies. Furthermore, it was suggested that regular theme sessions be organized for the General Assembly, that the Trusteeship Council be responsible for environmental questions and that the ICJ be strengthened, notably through the enforcement of its rulings based on Article 94 of the Charter. The Commission's proposals for the Trusteeship Council repeat Malta's views on the subject which had been announced more than five years earlier.

On reforming the Security Council, the Commission suggested phasing out the veto over 10 years and increasing its membership. However, it may be questioned to what extent this proposal is realistic for it seems unlikely that the 'permanent members [would] enter into a concordat agreeing to forgo its use save in exceptional and overriding circumstances'.[9]

The Commission was going one step beyond the other proposals creating new organs by explicitly calling for the abolition of ECOSOC and reviewing bodies such as UNCTAD and UNIDO. Although we are firmly opposed to discontinuing ECOSOC, we support the review of a few UN organs with the objective of finding their appropriate niche in the United Nations system. We are also sceptical with respect to the creation of an Economic Security Council since it could easily evolve into another restricted Security Council, depriving most countries of a democratic voice on economic, social and environmental matters.

Although the Commission on Global Governance recognized that many of its reform proposals could be achieved without amending the UN Charter, it still promoted a reformed Charter. The renewed legal document would then empower the international community with the possibility of intervention in domestic affairs for humanitarian and security reasons. A reform of the UN Charter would also serve to entrench the right of non-State actors to petition, thereby giving a voice to non-State actors. Yet reforming the Charter has, historically, proved to be a difficult

---

[9] The Commission on Global Governance, *A Call to Action*, Summary of *Our Global Neighbourhood*, Geneva, 1995; p. 15.

process. Thus, it is doubtful that the propositions of the Commission requiring structural and legal changes are likely to be implemented.

The South Centre has recently published its views and suggestions as they were presented at the forum on future United Nations reform in 1995.

In *Reforming the United Nations*, the South Centre insisted that any reforms be consistent with the fundamental principles entrenched in the Charter: democracy, accountability and respect for diversity.[10] In order to return to these principles, the Centre called for the implementation of various measures such as: a 'fully accountable' Security Council appointed by the General Assembly, further coordination between the specialized agencies, an Economic and Social Council responsible for economic security – possibly through the creation of an ECOSOC body in charge of policy and operational matters, more democracy within the Bretton Woods institutions, a unification of all agencies concerned with international economic policy (including the World Bank, IMF and WTO), and a regulatory body for transnational corporations. In addition, the South Centre favoured a revitalization of the international civil service conducted by an independent commission, as well as enhanced institutional and financial support for UNCTAD and UNIDO.

Before suggesting or agreeing to channel more scarce resources towards UNCTAD and UNIDO, we feel that the right niche for both entities has to be found. The South Centre's proposals also embodied another weakness. Whereas we share the Centre's concern for greater democracy within the United Nations, especially with respect to new sources of finance, we consider that the suggestions for achieving such a change tend to be disappointing. For example, in spite of calling for mechanisms to ensure that the arrears problem and the money-power link would vanish, the South Centre did not suggest concrete means to secure more financial democracy within the UN system.

In a further reform effort, the Independent Working Group on the Future of the United Nations put forward as its main proposal a restructuring of the Security Council and ECOSOC. The Group, in its report entitled *The United Nations in its Second Half-Century*, believed that a reformed United Nations would include

---

[10] *Reforming the United Nations: A View from the South*, South Centre, 1995; p. 23.

three councils – a new Economic Council, a new Social Council and a renewed Security Council – which would all be linked by a common Secretariat.

More specifically, the report suggested that a renewed Security Council have its membership expanded while the veto power be limited to Chapter VII or to any intervention involving the use of military personnel. In addition, it was suggested that a Security Assessment Staff be established to reinforce the early-warning system, coupled with the creation of an *ad hoc* military authority and UN rapid deployment force. The Economic Council would be responsible for integrating all United Nations organs concerned with economic issues and the Social Council would integrate the activities relating to social development. The Economic and the Social Council would be linked through a Global Alliance for Sustainable Development, that held yearly meetings at the highest level of government. Finally, the report also called for the creation of a working group to investigate alternative sources of financing for the Organization.

Although we agree with the report in its acknowledgement that there is a need to reform ECOSOC, we believe that to separate ECOSOC into two distinct Councils is not practical because, in any United Nations programme or intervention, separating the social from the economic component is not advisable. This would add to rather than reduce the United Nations task of co-ordination among its related activities. We believe that a Global Alliance for Sustainable Development, meeting once a year, would not be enough to provide this link between the social and economic activities of the United Nations system.

(c) Why is the United Nations System Still Not Meeting the Expectations of Member States despite the Myriad of Recommendations?

After this brief overview of the proposals for reforming the United Nations System, a question inevitably arises: with such a wealth of proposals and recommendations – and with probably more still to come – why have no significant proposals yet been implemented? Two factors, in our view, account for this situation. Firstly, previous reform proposals have involved major changes in the Charter, which is in practice a difficult goal to achieve.

Secondly, the lack of political will is another factor explaining the failure to implement reform proposals.

As mentioned above, most recommendations for reforms either tended to enhance the bureaucratic character of the Organization or created overlaps through the addition of new organs. In this regard, most of the reform proposals have overlooked one important criticism of the UN system: that its over-bureaucratized. Thus, by suggesting the creation of new organs, they hardly contributed to solving the fundamental problem of the Organization. Our suggestion focuses instead on streamlining and restructuring the Organization while at the same time reviewing some marginal organs and activities.

In addition, it has become clear that reforming the Charter of the United Nations is a considerable test of consensus for the sovereign nations of the world. Although there were several attempts to reform the Charter, particularly in the early years of the Organization, it was modified only twice on minor questions using Article 108.[11] Article 109 was never applied: the General Assembly and the Security Council never summoned a General Conference on reviewing the Charter. Moreover, it is unlikely that the proposals for reforming the Charter would survive the requirements of a two-thirds majority vote of the General Assembly in addition to the necessary unanimity of the Security Council Members. It follows that the previous reform proposals assuming a major reform of the Charter were unrealistic. Our proposals have to be seen in this context. They take this basic constraint into account and therefore do not require an immediate revision of the Charter.

The reform proposals so far did not only suffer from their shortcomings but were also victims of the hesitancy on the part of Member States. The United Nations can only be as efficient and as effective as its Members would like it to be. It has been obvious so far that a consensus has not been reached. The difference between rhetoric and practice has been and remains staggering. We should not underestimate the magnitude of the problem of reaching a consensus among the 185 Member States on such important matters as the expansion of the Security Council and the use of force in accordance with Articles 43 and 45 of the Charter.

[11] Spiry, Emmanuel, 'La réforme des institutions onusiennes: perspectives et prospectives (1985–1995)', *Studia Diplomatica*, No. 4, 1995; p. 9.

In these circumstances, we have no doubt that the only proposals and recommendations that will eventually be implemented will be those enjoying the support of all Member States. It is for this reason that, in our own discussions, ideas, and proposals, we have kept this sobering thought in mind and have endeavoured to be realistic and pragmatic whenever we were tempted to consider utopian alternatives.

FOUR

THE GENERAL ASSEMBLY AND ITS MAIN ORGANS: AN OVERVIEW OF THE PRESENT SITUATION

Summary

The aim of the present chapter is mainly to present the background for what we think should be the core of the new United Nations institutional framework, that is, the General Assembly and two of its main organs: the Economic and Social Council and the Trusteeship Council. The Security Council and the Secretariat and their mutual as well as respective relationships with the three above-mentioned 'principal organs' will be dealt with in chapter five. Therefore, the purpose of the present chapter will be to present the background for the General Assembly and its main organs, namely, how the present arrangements work. In so doing, we see that, even though the Assembly is the democratic and genuinely representative organ of the whole United Nations entity, the fact remains that it is neither efficient nor relevant and, moreover, does not have the role it deserves in the present United Nations order. As far as the two of its main organs are concerned, a distinction has to be made between ECOSOC and the Trusteeship Council: indeed, if the latter has obtained positive and highly useful results in its assigned area, that is, decolonization, the former has developed into a rather cumbersome body, plagued with institutional problems, and has been highly inadequate and inefficient in its role as a coordinating body within the United Nations system in the area of economic, social and related matters.

(a) *The General Assembly*

As can be seen from the following chapters, our proposals for the fiftieth anniversary of the United Nations have, as their institutional centrepiece, the General Assembly. Thus, before coming, in chapter five, to the proposed restructuring of this organ, we will first analyse the Assembly's present role in the United Nations and point out its shortcomings. We shall then similarly analyse the present position of two of its main organs aimed at assisting the Assembly in its tasks, namely ECOSOC and the Trusteeship Council.

Even though the General Assembly is today the only truly representative organ of the United Nations, the fact remains that, paradoxically, it is not efficient and relevant enough and, above all, does not have the role it deserves.

(i) A democratic and representative organ of the United Nations

According to Article 9(1) of the United Nations Charter: 'The General Assembly shall consist of all the Members of the United Nations'. Thus, among the six 'principle organs of the United Nations',[1] the Assembly is the only one that is really representative of the whole world community. It can even be argued that it is this particular organ which gives the United Nations its legitimacy. Indeed, as a consequence of the principle set out in Article 9(1), the Assembly is also an organ where all its members are, by definition, 'permanent members' in contrast, for example, to the Security Council, where only a few selected and powerful States are permanently represented. Of course, the five permanent members of the Security Council are also 'representative', in their own particular way – representative of a world order set up fifty years ago.

In contrast, States represented at the General Assembly are representatives of their Governments, and are not selected on the basis of their respective might, wealth or weight in the world. It can be argued that the General Assembly satisfies the primary

---

[1] According to Art. 7(1), these are: 'a General Assembly, a Security Council, an Economic and Social Council, a Trusteeship Council, an International Court of Justice, and a Secretariat.'

objective of a universal Organization: universality, especially universality in membership. According to Inis Claude:

> If the United Nations is conceived as a mechanism for perfecting a coalition against an identifiable hostile bloc, and perhaps also as a device for giving semi-global sanctions to the activities of such a coalition, a highly selective membership policy is obviously appropriate (...). If the Organization is to serve as the focal point for efforts to settle the disputes, moderate the attitudes, solve the problems, and eliminate the conditions which make for war and insecurity, its ranks should be as wide as possible. If the United Nations is to be a mirror of the real world, a forum for the consideration of the dangers that threaten and the challenges that confront the human race, an agency for dealing with the implications of interdependence, and an instrument for helping States to control their conflicts and collaborate in the pursuit of common interests, then maximum breadth of membership is essential.[2]

This, we agree, is in essence the nature and function of the United Nations that not only conforms most closely to the spirit of the Charter but also provides the most unique and promising role for the Organization. A role and an ideal that the United Nations has undoubtedly managed to achieve today, the Assembly being the living proof of that success.

Article 18(1) of the Charter states: 'Each member of the General Assembly shall have one vote', the rule: one State equals one vote, that is, the rule of absolute equality between United Nations Members, whatever their size, their wealth or their power, being at the basis of the democratic structure. Thus, remembering the great philosopher J.-J. Rousseau, we can say that if: one State equals one vote, then: equality equals democracy. To that extent, and to that extent only, unfortunately, can we say that the Assembly is just like a national parliament: 'If the contemporary international society were compared with a national State, the General Assembly could, with a little poetic licence, be held to represent the parliament in which the affairs of the world are debated and discussed by representatives of every region and

---

[2] Inis Claude, *Swords into Plowshares*, New York, Random House, 3rd ed., 1964; p. 91.

resolutions passed to decision-making bodies.'[3] And, after all, the comparison is not completely far-fetched.

The Assembly is a meeting place where the representatives of different regions gather to discuss common problems, like parliaments within States. It is called together at certain intervals, as parliaments were in earlier days. It allows the views which are widely held within the whole political society to be ventilated, as in a parliament. Its power of decision is small, like that of most parliaments until recently, but its voice carries, as theirs did, considerable moral authority.

However, the General Assembly is not, not yet at least, a 'world parliament' in any real sense. In particular, it is not representative of peoples in the way that an elected parliament is today supposed to be: it is representative of Governments, and these may or may not themselves represent accurately the views of their own populations.

What is meant by a 'world parliament'? Such an assembly would be composed of parliamentarians, these being designated by two possible means: first, they may be nominated – on the model of the Council of Europe's Parliamentary Assembly or of the European Parliament before 1979 – by their respective national parliaments, and then be sent to represent them in such a world parliament; the second is by a direct election, on the model of the present European Parliament: indeed, since 1979, European parliamentarians have been elected through universal suffrage. However that may be, we see that, unlike the present situation at the universal level, these two means to designate a world parliament involve, directly or indirectly, democratic elections – even though, at the global level, the first model (designation of parliamentarians by their national peers) would supposedly fit better than a system of direct and universal suffrage.

Thus, some authors have proposed the creation of a real 'world parliament' in order to make the United Nations a truly and genuinely democratic institution, these authors finding their inspiration in now rather outdated federalist perspectives: 'A federation is a government of peoples. Since the system of States members and action on States has proved ineffective, federalists argue that a supranational, or world government, vested with

[3] Evan Luard, *The United Nations – How it Works and What it Does*, New York, St Martin's Press, 2nd ed., 1994; p. 38.

powers to enact law binding on individuals must be created. Individuals would be made citizens of the world as well as national citizens. They would participate in the election of world representatives, and they would be subject to world laws just as to national laws.'[4] Some recent proposals for United Nations reform have advanced the idea of such a world parliament.[5]

However, even though the idea may appear attractive at first, we do not think it would be practicable in the circumstances as they presently apply to the General Assembly. Indeed, we do not see how this idea could be implemented in a world where a number of member countries still have limited experience in democratic elections, or in democracy *tout court*, most of the time. Thus, we favour the maintenance of a relative status quo; this status quo being characterized, as it has been developed above by (1) universality in membership,[6] and (2) the democratic rule: one State equals one vote.[7] Above all, we emphasize the idea of the pre-eminence of the General Assembly.

(ii) The General Assembly is not efficient and relevant and does not have the role it deserves

The General Assembly is primarily a discussion forum, with all the potential but, also, the pitfalls such as democratic organ implies. What does it discuss? Article 10 permits it 'to discuss any questions or any matters within the scope of the present

---

[4] Joseph Preston Baratta, *Strengthening the United Nations*, New York, Greenwood Press, 1987; p. 2.

[5] See chapter three and, in particular: Marc Nerfin, 'The future of the U.N. system', *Development Dialogue* 1985: 1; pp. 28–9; E. Childers and B. Urquhart, *Renewing the U.N. system*, Uppsala, D. Hammarskjöld Found., 1994; pp. 211–3.

[6] In this regard, it is worth quoting Baratta (*op. cit.*, p. 9): 'Universality is the great achievement of the U.N. Every weakness in the U.N. has been tolerated rather than tamper with the principle of universal membership, and every attempt to evict one country (. . .) has been rejected as a threat to the peace'.

[7] Some authors have attempted, in the recent past, to propose alternative voting solutions; Harold Stassen (*United Nations – A Working Paper for Restructuring*, Minneapolis, Lerner Pub., 1994; p. 12) is such an example. He proposes 'a continuation of a General Assembly of the U.N., with every sovereign State Member having a voice and vote, but with voting power to be proportionate so that a more realistic, democratic, and sensible scale of voting rights can be achieved'; he puts forward the idea that the specific number of votes of each member shall be established by taking into account three factors: 1. total population; 2. annual GNP; 3. annual per capita production. However, this solution would certainly not be as democratic as the present absolute and total equality between Member States.

Charter or relating to the powers and functions of any organs provided for in the present Charter.' The mandate could hardly be wider, as it encompasses almost anything under the sun which is of international significance, ranging from the world protein shortage to the definition of aggression. As the world becomes smaller and more closely interrelated, there is of course an increasing number of these questions which need to be discussed and decided internationally, from questions of peace and security to those in the field of trade, development, raw materials, human rights, disaster relief, decolonization and questions of international law. Most of these subjects the Assembly has regularly under its scrutiny. However, some of them are somewhat specialized questions and the General Assembly has therefore a number of separate committees where the different types of issues are discussed.

The First Committee is concerned with major political questions, especially disarmament. But it was soon decided that one committee could not cover these subjects adequately, thus an additional one was established: the Special Political Committee. This Committee dealt with major current political problems such as *apartheid*, the Palestinian problem, or the work of peace-keeping forces. The Second Committee deals with world economic and financial questions. The Third Committee is concerned with social, humanitarian and cultural matters: above all human rights. The Fourth Committee was originally concerned with Trust Territories but later was amalgamated with the Special Political Committee (resolution 47/233). The Fifth Committee is concerned with the Organization's budget and administration. Finally, the Sixth is concerned with questions of international law.

The problem stems from the fact that the various Committees act as alternative Assemblies, since every Member State is represented on each. This reduces their efficiency whenever they have to turn their attention to the legislative or supervisory work that the committees of an ordinary parliament would do ... though they occasionally set up small sub-committees of their own, thus reinforcing the phenomenon of institutional fragmentation inherent in the creation of a multiplicity of committees. Moreover, it is common knowledge that owing to the pressure on the plenary sessions it is often in the Committees that the most important debates take place. As one author states: 'The General

Assembly is a circus in which there is no guarantee that the main show will be going on in the centre ring.'[8] Thus, when the time comes towards the end of the session for the committees to report, debate in the plenary is often non-existent.

Therefore, the main problem we need to address when speaking about the internal functioning of the Assembly is that of institutional awkwardness and other institutional contradictions which – at the level they have reached today – constitute an obstacle to the smooth functioning of the whole institution and, thus, to the achievement of the Assembly's role as the legitimizing organ of the United Nations proper, as well as the democratic guarantee for the whole entity.

The General Assembly does not function to its potential as envisaged in the Charter. As already stated, the Assembly is not a world parliament in any real sense. It has no government. Member States are not committed to obeying the Assembly's decisions and resolutions. So the Assembly can discuss or recommend, but rarely decide. At most, therefore, 'the Assembly might be compared with a parliament of several centuries ago, composed of representatives of pocket and rotten boroughs, often varying grotesquely in populations, making occasional pleas to the powers that be, but exerting a decision-making authority which is at best extremely marginal,'[9] especially when compared with the powers given to the Security Council.

In fact, the *travaux préparatoires* of the Charter and, in particular, the Dumbarton Oaks Propositions reflect a clear intent to assign primary responsibility for problems of high politics and security to the Security Council, and to make the Assembly the supervisor of organizational housekeeping arrangements and activities in economic and social fields in order to avoid the overlapping and alleged confusion that attended the granting of wide and undifferentiated powers to the Assembly and Council of the League of Nations. To this end, the drafters of the Charter attempted to state with some precision the nature and scope of the Assembly's powers. Its functions were to discuss, to consider, and to recommend, but not to take action. This was to be the prerogative of the Council. In particular, as the detailed provisions regarding the powers and procedures of the Council in

[8] H. G. Nicholas, *The UN as a Political Institution*, London, Oxford Univ. Press, 4th ed., 1971; p. 107.
[9] Luard, *supra*, p. 38.

dealing with disputes and situations suggested, that organ was to have the primary responsibility for dealing with disputes and situations which endangered international peace and security.

At San Francisco, this allocation of powers came in for considerable criticism – particularly from small States – and a number of proposals were made for increasing the powers of the Assembly. These efforts met with a measure of success and as a result the Charter as finally drafted left the definition of the respective powers and responsibilities of the two organs somewhat unclear, thus opening the way to subsequent controversy and a substantial expansion in practice of the Assembly's powers and influence in the peace and security field. In particular, the Assembly has profited, during the whole period of the cold war, from the fact that the great-Power conflict minimized the institutional self-assertiveness and efficiency of the Security Council.

However, now that the direct East-West confrontation is over, the problem of institutional disequilibrium dating from 1945 has re-emerged as the Security Council has again assumed a predominant role in the United Nations institutional order. At the same time, since the end of the cold war, the General Assembly has seen its role and authority diminished.

With this evolution in mind, we believe it is time to address the problem of the authority of the Assembly's decisions or recommendations, which is linked with the two basic flaws of the Organization that we shall address in the following chapter: credibility[10] and, above all, legitimacy.[11] In this regard, one may say that, whereas Security Council resolutions based on Chapter VII of the Charter have a binding character, the General Assembly, even though it can discuss any imaginable topic, has no authority under the Charter to take binding decisions. Of course, since its inception, it has attempted to arrogate to itself such a power to take authoritative measures, but mostly in vain.

Indeed, after 50 years of United Nations practice, one may say that General Assembly resolutions or recommendations do have

[10] Indeed, what is the point in adopting resolutions which – as is well known – will not be implemented, as they are not given any binding effect by the Charter?

[11] We have seen that the General Assembly is the *locus* of the whole Organization's legitimacy: thus, rendering General Assembly resolutions mandatory would also enhance the legitimacy of the whole Organization.

a mandatory character in only three very precise and well-defined cases:

— first, when the content of the resolution is part of conventional law; but even in this case, it would only be binding on the States parties to the convention;

— secondly, a General Assembly resolution can repeat or be at the inception of a rule of customary international law; however, in that case too, one may identify a limit: indeed, such a rule would only enter general customary international law if it were confirmed by practice, such a resolution being only part of *opinio juris*;

— finally – and even more restrictively – a General Assembly resolution can have an immediate binding authority if it is an 'authentic interpretation' of a disposition of general international law and, in particular, of the Charter.[12]

Therefore – especially in the light of the Security Council's authority and present self-assertiveness – we believe that this situation should be urgently addressed by the international community. However, as the resolution of this anomaly – which endangers the general United Nations institutional equilibrium (with an impotent Assembly, and a powerful Security Council before it) – would necessarily involve a Charter reform,[13] propositions would be useless as long as the necessary consensus or political will was lacking on that point. However that may be, we repeat that it will not be possible to elude this important constitutional question much longer in the coming years, and that it will thus have to be confronted by the international community if the United Nations is to maintain its credibility and legitimacy.

(b) *Main organs*

With respect to economic and social matters and the problem of non-self-governing territories, the relation of the Assembly to the Councils, in comparison with that under the League system, was

---

[12] For the time being, the practice in this regard mainly concerns decolonization and the application of the right to self-determination, and the definition of 'aggression' (see, for example, Art. 39 of the Charter).

[13] Indeed, as these questions involve problems of institutional equilibrium and allocation of powers, we do not think the 'incremental way' to reform the Charter (see Spiry, Emmanuel, *loc.cit.* pp. 74ff.) would be envisageable or practicable here.

initially conceived as favouring the more representative organ. Whereas the League Council had important independent responsibility in these areas, the Economic and Social Council and the Trusteeship Council, while being given specific functions and powers, were expected to discharge their responsibility 'under the authority of the General Assembly'. In practice the Assembly has chosen to exercise this authority to the full, with the result that the Councils have come to resemble more closely subsidiary organs than the principal organs of the United Nations which the Charter declares them to be.[14] However, we prefer to call ECOSOC and the Trusteeship Council 'main organs' of the Assembly here, rather than 'subsidiary' or 'subordinate' organs.

(i) ECOSOC

In drafting the Covenant of the League, little attention was given to the economic and social foundations of peace; almost exclusive emphasis was placed upon the direct means by which war might be prevented. However, negotiators of the Charter favoured arrangements that would make the new organization more effective in this respect than the League had been. In particular, the proposals submitted by the American Government to the Dumbarton Oaks conferees, contained detailed provisions for economic and social cooperation, including a provision for an economic and social council which would have important quasi-executive responsibility. After initial objections by the USSR to broadening the scope of the proposed international organizations to include economic and social cooperation had been overcome, the Dumbarton Oaks conferees accepted in substance the American proposals. At San Francisco, the provisions of the Dumbarton Oaks proposals were even considerably expanded.

However, paradoxically, the Charter references to the economic and social functions of the Organization are ominously verbose, repetitive, and diffuse; largely because so many countries in 1945 refused to take these aspects of the United Nations seriously, nothing like as much care and attention was devoted to these clauses as to those which dealt with the purely political side of the Organization. Thus, from the beginning the Economic and Social Council was blurred in conception. Because by historical

[14] Art. 7(1), *op. cit.*

45

accident there already existed certain independent specialized agencies, ECOSOC was given the task of acting as a link with them; and because these same agencies fell very short of covering all the topics appropriate for United Nations treatment, ECOSOC was made into a kind of hold-all for the residue of specialist activities in the economic and social fields – as well as of some more properly to be regarded as political, e.g. 'the promotion of human rights'.

This dual nature of ECOSOC, part specialist agency, part 'super-agency', has made it much more difficult to establish a satisfactory relationship between it and the Assembly. Though explicitly said to be 'under the authority of the Assembly',[15] it has neither been given a free hand within a limited and subordinate sphere, nor obliged to confine itself to clear and manageable jobs in pursuance of an Assembly directive. In consequence the Second and Third Committees of the Assembly[16] have functioned more often as rivals to or duplicates of ECOSOC than as the broad policy-framers which they were intended to be. Thus, besides institutional inflation, there is another recurrent problem of the United Nations: overlapping and duplication. This phenomenon is particularly dramatic as far as ECOSOC is concerned. In this regard, we would emphasize the fact that the usefulness and relevance of the proposal made by some third world countries to transform the organ into a plenary body is rather doubtful as far as this problem is concerned. It would only institutionalize ECOSOC as another enormous talking shop, thus consecrating its total duplication with the Assembly itself. We believe there are other solutions which would make ECOSOC an efficient and useful organ, and we shall make concrete proposals on this question in chapter seven. We need to restore to this organ its original *raison d'être*: indeed, ECOSOC has fallen far behind the expectations of the Charter. Our proposals will tend to render it more effective and, thus, more relevant, as well as increasing coordination.

Indeed, as any careful analyst of the Charter might have expected – and encouraged as it was, by the loose language of the instrument, 'the infant ECOSOC began by pursuing every

---

[15] See Art. 66(1) of the Charter, which states: 'The Economic and Social Council shall perform such functions as fall within its competence in connection with the carrying out of the recommendations of the General Assembly.'
[16] See above.

economic and social objective in sight, with an extravagant faith in the virtue of words and resolutions and in the value of proliferating committees and commissions.'[17] However, fairness obliges one to add that some, at any rate, of the proliferation of commissions and sub-organizations was an expression of frustration on the part of poor nations which, having failed to interest the rich in directly ameliorating their plight, had had recourse to these fora as devices for publicizing, however inadequately, their problems and their poverty.

Nevertheless, although Member States may bear some responsibility for the way ECOSOC has grown and its subsidiary bodies have proliferated, the fact remains that this organ is totally inadequate as a coordinating instrument, especially as far as specialized agencies are concerned. It must be acknowledged that seldom have coordinating functions been described in more modest or tentative language: 'ECOSOC ... *may* coordinate the activities of the specialized agencies through *consultation* ... and *recommendations*;'[18] 'ECOSOC *may* take appropriate steps to obtain regular reports from the specialized agencies .... It *may* make arrangements ....'[19]

Thus, the phrases of the Charter reflect a continuously tender regard for the sovereignty and susceptibilities of international organizations, some of which antedate the United Nations and all of which have their own independent legislative organs, budgets, and secretariats. In consonance with this state of affairs, the Charter evaded the delicate task of defining the terms of the coordination and left this to be done in a series of subsequently negotiated agreements. Logically, it might be supposed that it would be with the negotiation of these agreements that ECOSOC's activities as coordinator would begin. But not only is the scope of coordination strongly limited, but paradoxically most of the coordination that does ensue is entrusted not to ECOSOC but to the Assembly and the Secretariat.

Therefore we shall endeavour, in chapter seven, to propose solutions to the main problems that we have identified which threaten ECOSOC's efficiency and, therefore, credibility, that is: first, a problem of overlapping, especially with some committees of the Assembly; and secondly, the failure of ECOSOC as a

[17] Nicholas, *supra*, p. 136.
[18] Art. 63, United Nations Charter.
[19] Art. 64; the emphasis is ours.

coordinating instrument, especially in its relationship with specialized agencies, including the Bretton Woods institutions.

(ii) The Trusteeship Council

The international trusteeship system is the successor to the mandates system of the League of Nations, but there are significant differences between the two. The mandates system – that is, the predecessor of the United Nations trusteeship system – applied only to specific territories detached from the Turkish empire and to Germany's former overseas possessions. The Covenant and the mandates agreements gave the League limited authority to supervise the administration of these territories. The trusteeship system was designed to cover a wider range of territories and gave the United Nations much greater powers. However, the principle that supervision of the management of mandated areas should be carried out by international organs was transferred from the League to the United Nations. The League Council and its auxiliary Permanent Mandates Commission were replaced by the Assembly and its subordinate Trusteeship Council.[20] The latter Council was designed as a body of governmental representatives in contrast to the independent expert membership of the Mandates Commission, and it was assigned a somewhat more elevated status in the organizational hierarchy than its prototype had enjoyed.

In fact, the powers of the Trusteeship Council are threefold.[21] The first is the right to submit questionnaires and receive reports from the administering Power. The second is the right to accept petitions from the area and examine them in consultation with the relevant Power. The third is the right to visit the territories periodically at times agreed upon with the administering authority. And, of course, there is implicit in all of these the right to debate matters which arise in any of these connections and to pass resolutions of a recommendatory character. Since it began to operate in 1946 the Council has been highly successful in maximizing its powers and making the best use of its opportunities. Its questionnaires became formidably elaborated. The replies

---

[20] Art. 85(2) of the Charter states that: 'The Trusteeship Council, operating under the authority of the General Assembly, shall assist the General Assembly in carrying out (its) functions.'

[21] They are enumerated in Arts. 87 and 88 of the Charter.

of administering Powers were then made the subject of cross-examination, written and oral. All this furnished material for a general debate, upon which was drawn up the annual report to the Assembly. The petitions from trust territories do not have to come via the administering authority, but can be submitted directly, and visiting missions can also receive petitioners.

Sometimes, visiting missions have seemed to cross the narrow line that divides supervision from administration, and administering Powers have dissented vigorously from courses of action which have been pressed upon them. In general, however, the tensions within the Trusteeship Council between administrators and their critics have been fruitful ones, producing on the one side many real improvements and on the other a gradual but perceptible shift away from mere 'anti-colonialism' to acceptance of a positive responsibility for the welfare and development of the territories concerned.

However, a hopeful image of trustful collaboration in the colonial sphere would prove as illusory as that of great-Power solidarity in the security sphere. Indeed: 'Mutual recrimination is more characteristic of the situation than mutual consultation. In retrospect, it is clear that what was achieved at San Francisco was not a compromise between colonial conservatism and anti-colonial radicalism, providing the basis for a collaborative approach to the tasks of trusteeship, but the creation of an arena within which the struggle of these two forces might be conducted.'[22] This is all the more regrettable as the Charter contained the seed from which genuine internationalization of trust territories might have grown, in its provision that the United Nations itself might serve as an administering authority.[23] This seed has, however, not been permitted to germinate, and States which have found themselves in possession and control of dependent areas have not been willing to abdicate in favour of an international regime. However that may be, this argument is more linked with the interested or concerned States' political will, and not with the Trusteeship Council's efficiency or usefulness as such.

Indeed, an objective evaluation of the trusteeship system would be rather positive in spite of the above criticism. First of all, the safeguards provided by the United Nations in this area

[22] Claude, *op. cit.*, p. 338.
[23] Art. 81, Charter.

have contributed to the reduction of colonial evils and abuses, and the pressures mobilized by international institutions have accelerated the process of economic, social, and political development in colonial areas. Similarly, the development of trusteeship has been remarkable in institutional terms. To use an analogy favoured by Inis Claude, the United Nations has assumed the role of a midwife, assisting at the birth of new States from the matrix of colonialism. It has functioned as a bureau of vital statistics, issuing international birth certificates to new claimants for membership in the world community. It has undertaken to exercise a tutelary function for newly independent States, helping them to develop the resources and master the arts which are essential for the meaningful enjoyment of national autonomy, and to acquire the habits and attitudes which are requisite for responsible participation in the affairs of an increasingly interdependent world.

This latter aspect of the Organization's work provides a compensatory mechanism for offsetting the effects of politically-induced premature birth of independent States. Thus: 'In the prevailing political climate, the U.N. has greater opportunity to promote the positive values of the concept of trusteeship in the post-natal period than in the pre-natal period of States. The ultimate record may show that the major contribution of the organization to the solution of the problem of colonialism lay in programs of assistance not explicitly related to the mechanisms for dealing with dependent peoples.'[24] It is precisely on this experience, not strictly related to the process of decolonization but to larger tasks of common interest, that our proposals for a revitalized Trusteeship Council will be based. These proposals for a Second Generation Trusteeship Council are presented in chapter six.

Finally, the United Nations trusteeship experience showed at least one important factor which should be kept in mind in our proposals dealing with economic and social reform (in chapter seven). Indeed, this experience – which has been, on the whole, one of the greatest achievements of the United Nations since its inception – points to the fact that without the Member States' political will, the decolonization process would never have been so successful – or, at least, would not have happened so quickly.

---

[24] Claude, *op. cit.*, p. 342.

Once political will was present, the United Nations was both relevant and effective in this area.

In contrast, in the economic and social areas, the Member States' political will is not sufficient and, thus, the whole United Nations still plays a very marginal role in those areas, the reason for this being rather simple: redistribution of wealth may not be in the interest of the richer countries, developed States agreeing to play the game and to be cooperative only as long as they benefit from it; thus, for instance, they will give financial aid to developing countries to the extent that most of the money will generally be spent in donor countries. This practice is as old as the United Nations itself, being the basis of the Marshall Plan launched in 1945 by the United States in favour of Europe. However that may be, the fact remains that we should retain this lesson from the past when considering the United Nations role in the economic and social spheres, in chapter seven.

FIVE

GUARANTEEING GLOBAL PEACE AND SECURITY: NEW ROLES FOR THE GENERAL ASSEMBLY, THE SECURITY COUNCIL AND THE SECRETARIAT

Summary

In our view, the Assembly does not deal effectively with problems of international peace and security: indeed, in this area, the Security Council has assumed a pre-eminent and, sometimes, exclusive role which we feel was not the initial intention of the framers of the Charter. Therefore, the pre-eminent – though not exclusive – role in the area of peace and security should be given to the Assembly. However, this transfer would also need to be accompanied by an enhancement, on the one hand, of the Assembly's credibility (by organizing – decennially or so – high-level summits of this organ) and, on the other, of the legitimacy of the whole United Nations (by the institution of an Assembly that meets on a continuous basis). Those alterations would necessarily have to be accompanied by some fundamental changes in the relation of the Assembly with the two other main United Nations 'principal organs', that is, the Secretariat and the Security Council. In particular, a 'new understanding' or a new 'division of labour' would have to be arranged between the General Assembly, the Secretary-General and the Security Council. This new arrangement would have two main features: first, a better definition and understanding of these organs' respective role in order to avoid any overlapping or competition among them; and secondly, an improved coordination between these institutions, the Secretary-General playing a major role in this regard.

(a) *Role of the General Assembly*

Malta, in its statement[1] at the forty-eighth session of the General Assembly declared: 'The approaching 50th anniversary of the United Nations provides an ideal opportunity for the international community to take an in-depth look at the means that it has at its disposal in its endeavours for peace, security and prosperity. This anniversary must be seen as an act of regeneration. It will highlight the universal richness and diversity of an institution which now encompasses practically the whole of mankind; it will rightly bring to the fore its qualities of resilience and perseverance which have been tested and demonstrated time and again over the half century; it will rightly recall the successes which have been achieved over the years, in spite of often daunting difficulties; it will salute the many individuals who have faithfully served and continue to serve, a few with great visibility and pertinence, most others quietly and silently out of the limelight. The process of regeneration must deal with institutions and objectives. Central to the institutional aspect is the role of the General Assembly.'

Indeed, it will be the objective of this chapter to present our proposals for this regeneration with the Assembly as the centre-piece of the United Nations system, before turning to our proposals for the two other main organs, the Security Council and the Secretariat.[2]

We believe that the proposals in this chapter as well as our other proposals can be implemented without major changes to the Charter. Moreover we believe that amendments to the Charter should not be an end in themselves, but only a means to a better United Nations. At present, we do not consider the difficulty in changing the Charter[3] to be a valid reason to forgo restructuring of the United Nations.

[1] Reprinted in: *Malta Review of Foreign Affairs*, Oct. 1993, pp. 1–11.
[2] As we have already noted, there are – according to Art. 7(1) of the Charter – six 'principal organs of the United Nations'. We will continue on the assumption that, the principle of free consent still being a fundamental feature of the jurisdiction of the International Court of Justice and, further, of the peaceful settlement of disputes at the international level, no change of this independent and autonomous body can be achieved without the consent and increasing efforts on the part of States to accept its jurisdiction and submit their disputes to this Court. Therefore, in the following paragraphs, we will mainly focus on three of the other main organs, namely the General Assembly, the Security Council and the Secretariat, beginning with the Assembly.
[3] For an in-depth analysis of the corresponding Chapter of the Charter and of the existing practice in this area, see: Spiry, E., *op. cit.*, pp. 65–70.

In our proposed new framework for a revitalized United Nations, the Assembly would strengthen its decision-making process, in particular through decennial summits held at the highest political level but also through regular meetings at the ministerial level: this would improve its *credibility* among Governments and international public opinion.

The second main concern is with the *legitimacy* of the Organization. This could be enhanced, as far as the Assembly is concerned, by the Assembly meeting on a continuous basis. A revitalization process is also needed within the Assembly itself, with regard to both its numerous Committees and to its President.

(i) Improving the credibility of the General Assembly: a decision-making process at the highest political level

If, as stated above, the idea of a world parliament is rather utopian, the will to introduce effectiveness, relevance and credibility into the work of the Assembly leads us to put forward the idea of summits held at the highest political level in order to involve statesmen, and not only diplomats, so that States would be obliged to commit themselves and take the Assembly more seriously than is their usual practice at the present time. Thus, the General Assembly must have more input into its work by Ministers and in some cases even by Heads of State or Government – transforming the role of visiting ministers, Prime Ministers and Presidents from the present one of honoured guests, to that of active and meaningful participants.

Summits should be organized every ten years or so at the Head of State or Government level to review the work that has been done by the Organization and its organs during the past decade and to determine what directions and general orientations should be taken by main United Nations organs in the years that follow.

The Assembly begins each year with the 'general debate', in plenary session, which is addressed mainly by foreign ministers, occasionally even by Prime Ministers or Heads of State.

Summits would not require a revision of the Charter; indeed, Article 20 reads: 'The General Assembly shall meet in regular annual sessions and *in such special sessions as occasion may require*. Special sessions shall be convoked by the Secretary-General at the request of the Security Council or of a majority of the Members of the United Nations.' In principle, the provisional agenda of a special session consists only of those items proposed for consideration in the request for the holding of the session. However, supplementary or additional items may be added by a two-thirds majority of those present and voting, as compared with the simple majority required at a regular session. Nevertheless, the fact remains that the Assembly is free to determine what items will be on its agenda in order to be discussed during those 'special sessions'. Moreover, under the Assembly's Rules of Procedure, any member may request that the Secretary-General summon a special session. The request is immediately communicated to all members and if a majority concurs within 30 days a special session is called.[4] The General Assembly itself may also 'fix a date for a special session'.[5]

The question arises as to the vote required for the calling of a special session. Normally, the Assembly operates on the basis of a simple or two-thirds majority of those present and voting.[6] In accordance with Article 20 of the Charter, however, it would seem that at least one half the entire membership of the Organization would have to give approval before a special session could be convoked.

However that may be, except perhaps on that last question of the majority required for the summoning of such a session, the Assembly can itself determine the rules governing such sessions, whether concerning their regularity, aims or length. Indeed, Article 21 states: 'The General Assembly shall adopt its own rules of procedure.' And, in contrast to the rules of procedure of other organs which have been infrequently changed, the Assembly's rules have been amended repeatedly, especially during the first ten years. The most important of these amendments were the revisions made in accordance with the 'Uniting for Peace' resolution of November 3, 1950 to enable the Assembly to meet, precisely in emergency special sessions. After passing that important resolution, the rules of procedure of the Assembly were revised to enable it, in particular, to meet on 24 hours' notice and to bypass a number of the usual procedures.

Most of the other changes have resulted from efforts to make

---

[4] Rule 9.
[5] Rule 11.
[6] See Art. 18 of the Charter.

the Assembly a more effective and efficient organ, and especially to cut down on the duration of Assembly sessions.

As far as the regular meetings at the ministerial level are concerned, the very same point as made above can be repeated, that is: nothing prevents the General Assembly, either in the Charter or in its rules of procedure, given the necessary political will, to institute such regular meetings in, say, its rules of procedure. Thus, as stated earlier, our proposals do not need application of Articles 108 and 109 of the Charter, that is, a formal and radical reform. To be adopted, such a reform would practically require unanimity whereas to apply our proposals would require only a consensus.

As stated, these summits would meet once every ten years or so and more frequently, at regular intervals, at the ministerial level. These summits would be a forum open to debate; the outcome of this debate would be unequivocal decisions and general directives to be followed and implemented by United Nations organs.

This new proposed organization of work at the Assembly level would be rather similar to the successful formula applied by the European Union, where summits of Heads of State are convened as needed to decide on political directions while regular meetings are organized at the ministerial level within the 'Council of Ministers'.

(ii) Towards a revitalized General Assembly

The Assembly is the only principal organ under the Charter wherein all Member States are permanent Members, and, regardless of size, power or wealth, have an equal and sovereign right, where all issues, political, economic, social, cultural or humanitarian, can be considered in their entirety and their interrelatedness, and where the process of decision-making may be conducive to consensus-building. In the light of this quasi-universal membership and its authority under the Charter, the Assembly constitutes the indispensable forum for international consensus-building, at the widest possible level, and can therefore make a unique contribution to the process of international peace and cooperation. Measures which would further reinforce, as well as highlight, the role of the Assembly in consensus-building therefore form an important aspect of its revitalization process.

The transformation of the Assembly into a plenary organ which meets on a continuous basis would be such a measure. The Assembly itself had attempted, in the past, to cut down on the duration of sessions. The very multiplicity of languages and words reveals one of the Organization's potential sources of strength and symbolizes the coming together of many peoples: namely the variety of humankind represented at the United Nations. It may be better that about 150 languages are being spoken, however stridently, all in the same building, than that they should be spoken in isolation from each other, in 150 separate corners of the earth. The hubbub of voices may not always be much listened to, but that they speak to each other at all shows that they are aware of others and concerned about their response. 'The barrage of words, the verbal duels and battles of paper may be wearisome and fruitless; but they are less dangerous and costly than a barrage of bullets, duels of tanks, or aircraft battles; and occasionally may help to make the latter less likely.'[7]

The fundamental function the General Assembly performs is indeed to make all more conscious of the attitudes and interests of others and so more inclined to take account of them. The Assembly is above all what its name implies: a meeting-place, where the nations can assemble and talk and discuss their problems with each other, and together deliberate and decide upon issues instead of each pursuing their own private destinies in total isolation as once they did.

The General Assembly would benefit if it were to meet throughout the year. There could be a first session (September to December), dealing exclusively with political and security matters; a second session on economic and related issues, a third annual session on humanitarian issues, a fourth one on human rights and related issues, and a fifth session on administration and finance.

Such a general framework would reduce the need for global conferences, which have tended to proliferate. We would not propose their elimination, however, as at times they still have a catalytic effect on the Assembly and its decision-making process.

[7] Luard, *op. cit.*, p. 57.

The Assembly should regularly meet at two different levels: at the working level on a continuous basis; it would then be composed of permanent representatives; and at the ministerial level in order to define the general orientations and tasks assigned to the other United Nations organs. This would need to be supplemented by a brief decennial summit (as discussed above) to give it the political will and legitimacy at the highest level.

At the working level, the permanent meeting of the Assembly could be decided, as in the case of the Ministerial sessions, by a simple resolution correcting or modifying the Assembly's Rules of Procedure.[8] Further, this change would only go in the direction that the Assembly has taken in practice. Indeed, it was originally thought that this institution would be able to complete its work in a five- or six-week session. These hopes were soon dashed. Under its own present rules, the Assembly is required at the beginning of each session to fix a closing date, but often has failed to finish its work within the prescribed time and has recessed, taking up at a resumed session those agenda items still not acted upon. Certainly, the drafters of the Charter did not intend that the Assembly should be in continuous session. However: 'There is nothing in the Charter or in the Assembly's Rules of Procedures to prevent one session of the Assembly from continuing until the next;'[9] and this has occasionally happened;[10] – in fact this is now more or less the general rule. An Assembly in session throughout most of the year would only follow a general trend, which should be institutionalized.

These changes are not enough. Difficult though it might be to achieve, some effort will need to be made to cut down on the proliferation of committees, meetings and staff which so damages the reputation, and depletes the resources, of the United Nations at present. Moreover, a leading role should be given to

---

[8] Under Rule 1 of the present Rules, sessions convene on the third Tuesday in September, although on occasion the opening has for various reasons been postponed.

[9] L. Goodrich, E. Hambro and A. P. Simons, *Charter of the United Nations*, New York, Columbia Univ. Press, 3rd ed., 1969; p. 182.

[10] The fifth, seventh, and eighth sessions were prolonged to enable the Assembly to deal speedily with any developments that might occur during the Korean conflict. The eleventh session was extended because of the Suez and Hungarian crises. The nineteenth session adjourned on 18 February 1965, until September of that year when it had its final meeting to receive the report of the Special Committee on peace-keeping operations, etc.

its President. The presidency of the Assembly is relevant to the structure and performance of the whole Organization. The role of the President should not only be that of presiding over the General Assembly, but also to represent it and to speak on its behalf on the basis of its decisions and resolutions.

The above-mentioned changes regarding the Assembly should also go hand in hand with a reorganized, stronger General Committee. This Committee consists of 28 members, no two of whom may be members of the same delegation, thereby ensuring its representative character. It comprises the President, and the vice-presidents of the Assembly, together with the chairs of the six main Committees. It is therefore composed of high-level personalities, and could have an important policy-making role. The General Committee studies the provisional agenda and the supplementary list, considers requests for the inclusion of additional items on the agenda, allocates items to committees, and submits its report for the approval of the Assembly. It also assists the President in drawing up the agenda for plenary meetings, determining the priority of agenda items, coordinating the proceedings of the committees, and in the general conduct of the work of the Assembly which falls within the President's competence. It may also make recommendations to the Assembly concerning the closing date of the session; but it may not, however, decide any political or substantive questions.

This role should be re-examined in order to make the General Committee a stronger organ, meeting continuously at the working level and at the ministerial level: thus, such proposals would be consistent with our above propositions concerning the Assembly itself. In fact, a strengthened General Committee would be necessary to ensure the effective operation of a reinforced General Assembly and to assist such an Assembly. Further, the Committee should be equipped to act on behalf of the General Assembly, with the capacity, for example, to field prompt fact-finding missions and with a degree of intervention capability sufficient to prevent crises from either starting or deteriorating. *Therefore, the General Committee should have a major role in the area of the peaceful settlement of disputes as well as peace-keeping.*

A new dynamic General Assembly and its subordinate organs would only be possible if there were more effective linkages through the President of the Assembly among the General Committee, the President of the Security Council and the Secretary-General of the United Nations.

(b) *Implementing the Decisions of the General Assembly: the importance of the Secretariat and the Security Council*

'The General Assembly is not, and cannot be seen as acting, either in contest or in competition with any other organ of the United Nations system. Its role is unique and pre-eminent and its deliberations can only facilitate, enrich and, as appropriate consolidate decisions in other organs.'[11]

There is a competitive or, at least, parallel competence with the Secretary-General in the area of the peaceful settlement of international disputes (Chapter VI of the Charter) and in the same way, with the Security Council which has, as its primary responsibility, the maintenance of international global security (Chapter VII of the Charter). A leading concept of the San Francisco Charter was that of the 'separation of powers' of the Assembly and the Security Council. However: 'In the actual operation of the United Nations, the breaking down of this concept of specialization has assumed the proportions of a major constitutional revolution. Gradually and increasingly, the Assembly has intruded into the Security Council's 'peculiar sphere'.'[12] It began by becoming a more frequently used alternative forum for the consideration of political disputes; it acquired the character of an organ of second recourse, an organ of appeal with relation to the Security Council; and, in the end, 'it has, in fact, virtually replaced the Council as the agency bearing primary political responsibility within the United Nations.'[13] The two organs' respective competence in the political and security area needs further clarification; thus, their collaboration would have to be improved. In particular, the Security Council should be more responsive and sensitive to the positions taken by the Assembly in this respect, in order to ward off criticism of the Security Council and the United Nations itself. Moreover, controversial decisions taken by the Security Council would gain wider acceptance if endorsed by the General Assembly.

[11] Declaration of Malta at the forty-eighth session of the General Assembly, *op. cit.*, p. 5.
[12] Claude, *op. cit.*, p. 161.
[13] *Ibid.*

(i) The Secretariat and the maintenance of international peace

The Secretariat is probably the major organ of the United Nations that has gone through most change and restructuring. Yet even today we hear criticism of its bureaucracy and its efficiency. The role of the Secretary-General is crucial and influences the work of the Secretariat as well as the way it is structured and functions.

The personal and professional qualities of the Secretary-General, therefore, are most important. Paradoxically, the Charter is rather vague about the selection and appointment. Article 97 states that: 'The Secretary-General shall be appointed by the General Assembly upon the recommendation of the Security Council.' This provision was approved at San Francisco following insistence by the major Powers that the vesting of important political responsibilities in the Secretary-General required that the Security Council be given a decisive part in the choice of a person to fill the office. It was emphasized that if the Secretary-General were to be effective in his political role, he would need to have the confidence of the major Powers. However, the fact that essentially the Secretary-General is chosen by the five permanent members of the Security Council calls into question the credibility of the relevant Articles of the Charter.

The use of the word 'appointed' in Article 97 instead of 'elected' shows that the office was conceived at the time as being primarily – though not exclusively – an administrative office. Even if this were the case in 1945, the Secretary-General's role as it has developed today is obviously not that of an international administrator. His role is certainly more political, and he is now more a diplomat than a mere administrator. One would like to see the Assembly play a more prominent role in his selection. In the second place, it may be argued that even in 1945, the drafters of the Charter did not intend to give the Secretary-General the role of a pure administrator. Indeed, when the United Nations was established, it was always intended that he should play a more prominent role than the Secretary-General of the League. Some even wished him to be a kind of super-statesman, a world conciliator and arbitrator. President Roosevelt believed he should be called the 'World's Moderator', who would seek to mediate all the great conflicts that arose. And many others felt that he should at least be given greater powers of initiative than the somewhat anonymous League Secretary-General had had. For this reason the Secretary-General of the new body was vested with a new authority: the power to raise matters which he thought should receive the attention of the Organization.

Under Article 99, he was enabled to 'bring to the attention of the Security Council any matter which in his opinion may threaten the maintenance of international peace and security'. Subsequently, under the rules of procedure of the Assembly, he was also given the right to put an item on the agenda of the Assembly or to 'make either oral or written statements to the General Assembly concerning any question under consideration by it'. In this way, he acquired the right of initiative, both in the Council and the Assembly. In addition to this, he was to perform 'such other functions as are entrusted to him' by the Assembly, the Security Council or other councils of the Organization (Article 98); thus, these organs have entrusted innumerable particular tasks to him. In order to execute these assigned tasks properly the Secretary-General should be assisted by three Deputy Secretaries-General: one for Political, Security and Peace Affairs; one for International Economic Cooperation and Sustainable Development, and another for Administration, Management and Conference Services.

Among the functions entrusted to the Secretary-General by the different principal organs, it is certainly by his role in the area of peaceful settlement of disputes and, more generally, in the sphere of the maintenance of international peace, that he exerts most influence. This is an area in which the two other organs – Security Council and Assembly – are very much involved today. These have to work together and to coordinate their respective positions. The Secretary-General should have a central role in the identification of a common United Nations position on questions dealing with the maintenance of international peace and security, in particular, concerning the pertinence of sending peace-keeping forces to a particular country.

Indeed, in addition to being chief executive and administrator of the United Nations, the Secretary-General has important functions and powers as coordinator of the policies and activities of United Nations organs. The Secretary-General's responsibility for coordination are nowhere explicitly stated in the Charter. They derive from resolutions passed by the Assembly which request him to undertake various tasks. This position as coordinator of policies and activities of the United Nations should be improved and strengthened, especially as far as his relation with the Assembly and the Security Council are concerned.

The Secretary-General need not and should not be the only one to play the role of 'go-between' or 'honest broker' helping to coordinate positions on questions of common interest, in particular as far as peace and the peaceful settlement of disputes are concerned. The role of the President of the Assembly as co-ordinator – more specifically with the Security Council and the Secretary-General – should also be developed.

In the United Nations, as in the League, the convention has become firmly established that the President of the Assembly should not be a representative of a permanent member of the Security Council – and this tradition should be maintained. This facilitates the President of the Assembly acting as a coordinator, with the Security Council and the Secretary-General as well as a consensual figure able to smooth out areas of dissension within the Assembly itself.

This well-established tradition has not prevented the office from attracting the services of some of the leading figures of the international scene. From the first President, Henri Spaak of Belgium, onwards the presidency has been well served by its incumbents. Though the powers of the President are limited, personal influence can do a great deal to expedite the work of a session and to maintain the interests of the Organization against undue partisan pressure of any of its Members. These personal qualities would be all the more important in the context of a continuous Assembly, as earlier proposed.

(ii) The Security Council and the maintenance of international security

'The Security Council is a unique tool in the search for peace and security. It forms a blend of the idealistic and the pragmatic; it is at one and the same time a deliberative as well as a functional organ. The lifting of the cold war constraints has had a most visible and creative impact in the way it has released and galvanized the peace-making and peace-keeping roles of the Security Council.'[14]

We know that the Security Council has a privileged – though

---

[14] Declaration of Malta (48th session of the General Assembly), *op. cit.*, p. 6.

not exclusive – competence in the area of Chapter VII, that is, collective security. Thus, the first idea would be to give this organ the necessary means for its action: mainly an effective and efficient Military Staff Committee. However, the *sine qua non* condition and the necessary parallel to this increase in the Security Council's coercive instruments would be an internal reform of the organ in order to make it more democratic or, at least, to enhance its legitimacy and ensure that its decisions are well-founded.

We do not particularly favour the idea launched in 1988 by Brian Urquhart, and subsequently taken up by Boutros-Ghali in his *Agenda for Peace*,[15] that is, the concept of a permanent United Nations army or military contingents which would be permanently available to the United Nations. Beside the fact that it is not new – indeed, the Charter itself, in its Article 43, contains such an idea – the concept is neither feasible nor realistic. To quote E. Luard: 'The machinery proposed in Article 43 of the Charter for a Security Council force raised many hopes, but was probably always unworkable. Even if it had been possible to reach agreement on the composition of the force, it would almost never have been possible to use it. For one permanent member or another would almost always have been fearful that this might have been to the disadvantage of its own side or interests, and so have used its veto.'[16]

Of course, one could contend that such arguments have been untenable since the ending of the cold war. Yet it is noteworthy that Article 43 was not invoked even against Iraq in 1990–91. In fact, in the present international environment, the problem with a permanent United Nations force would be exactly the same as in the case of peace-keeping: it is not because some countries are particularly keen on United Nations peace-keeping that they will accept to send their troops in a particular situation. For example, no country was ready to send national contingents to either Rwanda or Haiti; thus, some permanent members of the Security Council, whose behaviour is necessarily motivated either by national prestige or strategic considerations (or both) finally decided to intervene there.

That being so, ambitions regarding the implementation force put at the disposal of the Security Council have to be lowered.

---

[15] General Assembly-Security Council, U.N. Doc. A/47/277, 17 June, 1992.
[16] *Supra.*, p. 30.

We would propose a more practical and certainly more useful solution, that is, the introduction of an effective and representative Military Staff Committee. Indeed, it should be noted that the 'failure [to set up an effective Military Staff Committee] left the Security Council with a central part of its system of peace-enforcement totally inoperative.'[17] Therefore, such a Committee[18] would have a primary role in directing peace-keeping operations and troops, and would be responsible, not only for the military aspects of the operations in the field, but also for the safety and well-being both of the forces deployed and of the inhabitants of the areas concerned. However, it should be noted that this kind of United Nations peace-keeping operation should only be of the 'advance' or 'emergency' kind; indeed, in our view, larger, and long-term operations would need to be decentralized to regional Institutions like OSCE.

To return to the central (collective) security system at the universal level and to the above-mentioned idea of an effective – and, thus, relevant – Military Staff Committee, it should be noted that the idea had already been put forward by the Government of Malta as early as 1983, in the '19 Points' (presented by the Maltese representative at the Security Council). This informal document envisaged, among other elements, that such a measure as 'activating the work of the Military Staff Committee' could usefully be considered.[19] Several years after the '19 Points', we still believe that this measure would be useful, in particular in cases where peace-keeping operations need to be coupled with military operations in the field. In such cases, indeed, coordination between peace-keeping and coercive action is absolutely essential if losses of 'Blue Helmets' are to be avoided.

In a statement to a Working Group of the Security Council on 22 February, 1995, Malta declared: 'The primary aim of any measure of reform, be it in terms of composition or working method, should be an enhanced legitimacy for Security Council decisions.'

One of the important objectives of any enlargement of the Security Council's membership, must be an effort to ensure balance and equity in its composition in terms of the present increased United Nations membership. Account must be taken

---

[17] Nicholas, *op. cit.*, p. 79.
[18] See Art. 47 of the Charter.
[19] Quoted in: *Malta Review of Foreign Affairs*, No. 6, January 1995, p. 44.

of regional and geographical considerations, and of the need to provide reasonable opportunities for all Members to take their turn in serving on it. Further considerations relate to the size and status of individual United Nations Members.

Indeed, in the past 50 years, membership has more than trebled. An increase in the Security Council to around 25 members is today not only justified but desirable. There appears to be a broad consensus on the need to increase Security Council membership. Differences still exist on the extent and type of such an expansion, foremost amongst which is the discussion as to whether an eventual growth in membership is to be coupled with an increase in the number of States holding permanent member status.

The original distinctions in the composition of the Council are the fruit of the historical context in which they were drawn up. The selection of permanent members would necessitate the identification of new, objective criteria to determine qualification. Such criteria can only be based on factors which may change over time – *non-permanent* factors on which *permanent* membership is decided. However, history teaches us that realities change. Circumstances have altered over the past 50 years and will inevitably continue to evolve. This is where the difficulty lies.

Another key issue in the debate on the restructuring of the Security Council is that related to the permanent members' right to *veto*. Since its inception at the San Francisco Conference 50 years ago, the veto system has remained the subject of deep divisions within the international community. The veto system has been used, ill-used and abused, as is well known. For this reason, we welcome the prevailing post-cold war mood in the Security Council whereby permanent members generally desist from using the veto. Building on this new pattern of non-exercise of the right to veto decisions we can augur a future Council which would be more open in its decision-making process, more representative in number, less dependent on a veto situation, but moving towards a proper, qualified majority in its decisions. We believe that it would be prudent to dilute the right to veto somewhat by requiring at least two negative votes from the existing five permanent members to block the passage of a resolution.

The Italian proposal to introduce quasi-permanent members of the Security Council deserves consideration because it involves a larger number of States participating on a criteria basis and seeking to ensure thereby a more equitable representation.

Another useful means to enhance the maintenance of international peace and security would be the endorsement of *regional conferences on security*. Thus, in the year following submission of the '19 Points' to the Security Council in 1983, Malta's Permanent Representative prepared some additional proposals to facilitate the work of the Council. Among them was the following: '6) The Security Council should follow with interest, encourage, and even endorse or assist regional initiatives to prevent conflict.'[20] Indeed, an aspect which requires redefining in its application is that of regional responsibility for peace-keeping in terms of Chapter VIII of the Charter. Malta's proposal at the CSCE follow-up meeting in Helsinki, namely that the CSCE declares itself the regional arrangement in terms of Chapter VIII of the Charter, was endorsed by the Helsinki Summit II. We consider that, through similar arrangements on regional levels, peace-keeping operations may be more efficiently dealt with by such countries which, because of their regional obligations, can assume further responsibilities.

These efforts at regionalization have increased in recent years and one can only hope that this trend will continue and be consolidated, and that the Security Council will agree to actively encourage it. It is only natural that Malta attach relevance to the Mediterranean region – a region suffering the turmoil caused by the problems in its midst. The importance of having its environment safeguarded, the relevance of its sea routes and its strategic role in linking three continents are all factors with consequences extending far beyond the boundaries of the region. Aware of this situation, Malta has shown continued interest and involvement in promoting Mediterranean cooperation. It has supported the proposal for a conference on security and cooperation in the Mediterranean and proposed the setting up of a Council for the Mediterranean as a forum for political, economic and social dialogue in the region. In addition, in March 1995, in Paris, at the final conference of the Pact on Stability in Europe, Malta launched the proposals for a Stability Pact for the Mediterranean, developing the idea further in Barcelona during the Euro-Mediterranean Conference in November 1995. The Stability Pact for

[20] *Ibid.*, p. 47.

the Mediterranean would create the modalities for dialogue in the region and seek to establish mechanisms to prevent crises escalating into conflict. Within the framework of the Barcelona process, it would formulate a series of agreed measures which could contribute towards the progressive reduction of tension and lead to the building of mutual confidence and understanding among Mediterranean States.

SIX

THE TRUSTEESHIP COUNCIL: A MALTA INITIATIVE WHOSE TIME HAS COME

Article 88[1]
The Trusteeship Council shall hold in sacred trust the Principle of the Common Heritage of Mankind. It shall monitor compliance with this principle in accordance with international law, in Ocean Space, Outer Space, the atmosphere as well as Antarctica and report any infringement thereof to the General Assembly and/or CCSSD. It shall deliberate on its wider application to matters of common concern affecting comprehensive security and sustainable development and the dignity of human life, and make its recommendations to the authorities and institutions concerned. The Trusteeship Council shall act as the conscience of the United Nations and the guardian of the future generations.

Elisabeth Mann Borgese
Ocean Governance and the United Nations

Summary

We have seen, in chapter four, that the Trusteeship Council has served its purpose in terms of the Charter. But its very success in bringing to nationhood so many countries and peoples previously under trust has considerably diminished its role.

[1] Revised Article 88 of the UN Charter as proposed in the book *Ocean Governance and the United Nations*, Part III, entitled 'The United Nations 2020', by Elisabeth Mann Borgese, Center for Foreign Policy Studies, Dalhousie University. In the Explanatory Notes (p. 240), the author recognizes that the idea of the Trusteeship Council being dedicated to this great new purpose now that its task of decolonization has been completed, was proposed by the Minister of Foreign Affairs of Malta in his concluding address as President of the General Assembly in 1991.

However, we believe that this institution is still relevant today and that the initial philosophy present at its inception is universal in time and in space – that is, the idea of holding in trust some shared or common values of mankind and humanity. Thus, we propose, instead of simply discontinuing this organ, to reinterpret (extensively) its mandate; we suggest that the Trusteeship Council should hold in trust for humanity its common heritage and its common concerns: the environment; the protection of the extra-territorial zones and the resources of the sea and of the seabed; the climate and the rights of future generations, as well as the rights of peoples in situations where there has been a complete breakdown of the State. This seems to be a feature of the post-cold war era with which both the General Assembly and the Security Council seem to be unable to deal. Of course, this major extension in the Trusteeship Council's mandate would have to be accompanied by a new definition of the organ's place in the United Nations institutional order; i.e. a more clearly structured hierarchical position *vis-à-vis* the Assembly and enhancement of its role as a body coordinating United Nations activities in the areas under its trust. Malta's position was submitted to Member States in an *aide-mémoire*, reproduced as Annexe II on page 142.

(a) *An Extensive Reinterpretation of the Mandate of the Trusteeship Council*

Article 85(2) of the Charter reads: 'The Trusteeship Council, operating under the authority of the General Assembly, shall assist the Assembly in carrying out (its) functions'. In particular, we would like to see the Assembly reorient and broaden its mandate towards a wider purpose than the one for which it was originally created: it should hold in trust the common heritage and common interests of mankind, mainly: environment, sea, rights of peoples, human rights, and take charge of the implementation of the decisions adopted and directions taken in these areas by the Assembly. Finally the new Trusteeship Council should also act as a coordinating body between the different United Nations organs whose aim and purpose is, precisely, to act and intervene in such areas as human rights or the rights of future generations.

Before discussing the new extended mandate that we should

like to see accorded to that organ, we wish to show that such an extension could be achieved with only minor amendments, if any, to the Charter.

(i) Feasibility of the proposal to extend the Trusteeship Council's competence

In our view, two sets of arguments may be advanced.

First, the new, extended mandate of the Trusteeship Council accords with the basic *philosophy* underlying the creation of that organ. In fact, the basic assumption made was that colonialism is one of the factors making for war in the modern world; hence: 'trusteeship is justified in terms of the general war-prevention function of international organizations'.[2] This concept was formally stated when the drafters of the Charter listed the furtherance of international peace and security as the first of the 'basic objectives' of the special trusteeship system to be created under the auspices of the new organization.[3] Thus, as the idea of 'trust' or 'trusteeship system' is linked to the maintenance of peace and security, and can be interpreted as a means to maintain them, this provides us with a very broad and general basis for the Trusteeship Council: its aim is far wider and deeper than just decolonization.

To that extent, we believe that the basic philosophy underlying the setting up of the Council is one which viewed colonialism as both a symptom and a case of an unhealthy situation in the global body politic. In this analysis, war is a result not so much of conflicts as of conditions; it is treated as an outgrowth of circumstances rather than an act of policy. Peace is a function of a healthy society, in which all component groups enjoy justice and basic human rights, share in a mutuality of respect, participate in the values of economic and social progress, and move towards political maturity. 'This ideal cannot be reached so long as the system of colonial overlordship keeps the map spotted with blighted areas, inhabited by peoples which are denied both the advantages and the responsibility of full citizenship in the human commonwealth.'[4] Hence, the task of trusteeship is to help make the world fit for peace by launching a kind of international

---

[2] Claude, *op. cit.*, p. 318.
[3] See Art. 76.
[4] Claude, *op cit.*, p. 320.

slum clearance project, and promoting the progressive development of peoples that have been left behind or regulated to the rear, in particular in such basic areas as human rights, rights of peoples or respect for their most immediate human environment.

Thus, we believe that the philosophical and moral bases of the Trusteeship Council are very broad, and that the proposed extension of its competence would be perfectly in line with these bases.

Secondly, this interpretation is corroborated by the *practice* of the United Nations in the area of 'trust' territories. Indeed, if we observe and analyse the overall evolution, beginning with the League, we would see that the whole trusteeship system has constantly evolved in the sense of larger mandates and purposes. The requirements of the United Nations are evolutionary in concept, answering to the dynamism of world events, calling for a revised response to altered situations. In our view, nothing should obstruct this evolution, not even (if necessary) the legal complexities of amending the Charter.

Thus the evolution of the trusteeship system is noticeable as far back as 1945, when we compare the Charter with the Covenant of the League; indeed: 'In defining the basic purposes of the trusteeship system, the Charter [went] far beyond the provisions in the Covenant of the League of Nations.'[5] The purposes of the League mandates system were not brought together in one place or stated in generalized terms. The well-being and development of 'peoples not yet able to stand by themselves under the strenuous conditions of the modern world' were recognized as general overall purposes in Article 22 of the Covenant. And, in Article 23(b), League members further undertook 'to secure just treatment of the native inhabitants of territories under their control'. Nevertheless, this unenforceable expression of good intent was the only mention in the Covenant of colonial peoples, except for those who having lost their wartime masters were put under the mandates system.

The Charter, by contrast, contains a lengthy 'Declaration Concerning Non-Self-Governing Territories' (Chapter XI). This, admittedly, is no more enforceable than the Covenant's Article but its range and precision create a stronger moral pressure

[5] Goodrich and Hambro, *supra.*, p. 467.

on Members. In place of the indefinable 'just treatment' of the Covenant we have a recognition that the interests of the local inhabitants are to be paramount, that their political, as well as economic, social, and educational advancement is to be ensured, that 'self-government' is to be developed, that 'constructive measures of development' are to be promoted and 'research' encouraged; and so on and so forth. To quote H. G. Nicholas: 'these clauses undoubtedly represent the admission of a new concept – the claim of an international organization in principle to interest itself in the affairs of dependent peoples, *even those who do not come under the umbrella of its mandates.*'[6]

However, if an extension of the mandate in the area of 'trust territories' is noticeable when compared with the League's treatment of such areas, one can also notice an extension, in practice, of the initial United Nations mandate. This extension has more particularly been operated through the action of the Assembly and, more specifically, of its Committee on Information on Non-Self-Governing Territories. This body, which grew by degrees out of an *ad hoc* committee of the General Assembly set up in 1946 and a three-year 'Special Committee' set up in 1947, came to establish itself as a potent and continuing Assembly organ. It paralleled the Trusteeship Council in its style of composition, equal numbers of administering (i.e. colonial) and non-administering States. 'All in all the Committee's rise as a parallel body to the Trusteeship Council constituted a *forceful instance of the Assembly's capacity to respond to novel demands.*'[7]

Nor did the development stop here. In 1960, the General Assembly adopted unanimously the Declaration on the Granting of Independence to Colonial Countries and Peoples. This made colonialism *per se* improper, and this Declaration – almost an amendment to the Charter – provided a platform for further pressure. Alleging that it was being ignored, the activists established a new committee, the Special Committee on the Situation with Regard to the Implementation of the Declaration on the Granting of Independence to Colonial Countries and Peoples, the 'Committee of 24'. It was directed by the General Assembly to employ 'all means' to do its job and, in 1963, to this end was

[6] *Op. cit.*, p. 30. The emphasis is ours.
[7] *Ibid.*, p. 149; our emphasis.

authorized to take over all previous committees' work, including that of the Committee on Information.

Overall, this evolution shows that the Assembly – if and when it is animated by sufficient political will[8] – can transform the existing institutions put under its authority by the Charter and allot them new, precisely defined tasks. In particular, nothing prevents the Assembly from making the Trusteeship Council more responsive to its decisions and, thus, to totally redefine its aims and purposes – given the political will. We believe that this prerequisite can be met today, as some positive governmental reactions to Malta's initiative to revitalize the Trusteeship Council show. It should be noted that this initiative, which was formalized in June 1995,[9] led to the placement of this important item on the agenda of the fiftieth session of the General Assembly. It will then be discussed by all interested States; in the context of the ongoing discussions on the reform of the Organization.

(ii) From decolonization to the protection of the 'common heritage' of mankind

The last territory remaining under the trusteeship system was the Trust Territory of the Pacific Islands. On 22 December 1990, by resolution 683, the Security Council agreed to the termination of the trusteeship in respect of three of the four component parts of the Trust Territory of the Pacific Islands, i.e. the Federated States of Micronesia, the Marshall Islands and the Northern Mariana Islands. Following the November 1993 plebiscite in which the people of Palau freely exercised their right to self-determination, the Trusteeship Agreement of this last remaining territory under the trusteeship system came to an end. Therefore, on 25 May 1994, the Trusteeship Council adopted an amendment to its Rules of procedure establishing that it would henceforth meet as and where the occasion might require by its

---

[8] We remind the reader that Malta proposed the idea of decennial high-level political summits of the General Assembly as well as more regular meetings at the ministerial level to adopt current decisions, in order to strengthen the Assembly's political will and enhance its credibility; see chapter five.

[9] See Letter dated 2 June 1995 from the Permanent Representative of Malta to the United Nations addressed to the Secretary-General, UN doc. A/50/142, 16/06/95.

own or its President's decision, or at the request of a majority of its members, the General Assembly or the Security Council.

The Secretary-General, in his report on the work of the Organization, has recommended that the Assembly proceed with steps to eliminate this organ in accordance with Article 108 of the Charter, which provides for amendments to the Charter to be made by two-thirds majority of the Assembly including the Permanent Members of the Security Council.

However, before proceeding with such a recommendation, it is our belief that other alternatives need to be considered amongst which is the recommendation to transform and focus the mandate of the Trusteeship Council entrusting it with the responsibility of safeguarding the common heritage of mankind. 'Within the concept of a Second Generation United Nations, we have put forth a proposal to further activate and give an added role to the Trusteeship Council. It is a Council that has served the Organization in dealing with territories in its trust, most of which today are valid Members of the United Nations. The Council's present diminished relevance is in fact a reflection of its own success. Yet, the concept of trusteeship lies at the very core of our Organization.'[10]

Malta served as President of the forty-fifth session of the Assembly from September 1990 to September 1991. It was during Malta's tenure of office that it first launched the idea of transforming the role of the Trusteeship Council. We should like to emphasize the fact that, since the idea was launched by Malta, several authors and organizations have incorporated it into their own proposals.[11]

The proposal was introduced at a time when the international community was emerging from the grip of the cold war, at a time when it was becoming clearer to all that notions of security

---

[10] Malta representative, forty-eighth session of the General Assembly, *op.cit.*, p. 9.

[11] Two examples can be given here: first, E. Childers and B. Urquhart (*op. cit.*, pp. 201–2), who proposed in 1994: 'Initially by its powers under Art. 22, and in the next Charter revision process by amendment of Chapters XII and XIII to reformulate the Trusteeship Council, the General Assembly should establish a United Nations Council on Diversity, Representation and Governance', with extended functions in the area of human rights. The second, more recent example is the project submitted by the Commission on Global Governance (*A call to Action – Summary of Our Global Neighbourhood*, Geneva, 1995, p. 15), which states that: 'The Trusteeship Council should be given a new mandate over the global commons in the context of concern for the security of the planet.'

no longer stemmed solely from military considerations. In fact, it clearly appears today that we cannot aspire to a new world order and yet persist in viewing the United Nations institutional mechanisms through those same cold war lenses, ill-focused for our times and shattered by the course of history. We need to view the United Nations as a complex, adaptive system. A system which, without renouncing its original ideals and basic purposes, responds adequately and promptly to contemporary needs. A proactive United Nations rather than a reactive one.

And, in line with what we have stated above on the wide basis of the trusteeship system as a means to prevent war, the progressive disappearance of resources at present and in the future, the sustainability of the environment, the promotion of human rights and safeguard of peoples in situations of complete breakdown of the State, constitute challenges to human security and the well-being of present and future generations.

The United Nations is mandated to ensure that present and future generations benefit from and enjoy peace in freedom. This worthy goal necessitates flexibility in the functioning of the United Nations system, and review and revitalization of existing organs, hence the Maltese proposal to transform the Council from a guardian of dependent territories to one which acts as guardian and trustee of the global commons and the common concerns in the interest of present and future generations.

The concept of the 'common heritage', first launched by Malta at the United Nations in 1967, has today acquired universal acceptance which has led to its incorporation in a number of international conventions. The concept of the common heritage of mankind, revolutionary when first launched, remains an appealing one today. It is a concept which brings contemporary notions of space and time together. More importantly, it provides an inherent link to the past as well as an opening to the future, a new dynamic which helps overcome a static world view. The notion of a heritage informs the logic necessary for wider parameters in the assessment of the here and now. It has stimulated a world vision which no longer concentrates solely on present-day situations but transcends self-interest and examines issues beyond our immediate human condition. It is a measure of the inter-generation solidarity for which we all strive in the creation of a truly dignified humanity.

The essence of the concept of common heritage is trust. The

Trusteeship Council when first formed incorporated this notion of trust. To quote Malta in its statement to the 49th session of the Assembly (30 September, 1994): 'The concept of trust ... is one which reflects the mission of the League of Nations and later the United Nations in so far as certain territories were concerned. We have to apply the concept of trust to new realities. We believe that the United Nations holds in trust for humanity its common heritage and its common concerns: the environment, the resources of the sea and the seabed, the climate, the rights of future generations and the safeguarding of the rights of peoples in situations of complete breakdown of the organs of the State. We believe that we hold these in trust for humanity and an enhanced and redefined Trusteeship Council can be the right organ for this purpose.'

(b) *A Newly defined Niche in the United Nations Institutional Order for the Trusteeship Council*

This newly defined niche can be underlined by two characteristics: first, the new Trusteeship Council would be entrusted with a new *ratione materiae* competence, mainly encompassing what we know today as the promotion of human rights and the protection of the human environment, these two areas being intimately related to each other: indeed, where is the human dignity and well-being in a spoiled and polluted environment?

The second area where an in-depth transformation of the present Trusteeship Council's mandate is necessary for it to achieve its goals and, in particular, to be a useful and efficient organ protecting human rights and the human environment, is in its relationship with other United Nations organs, mainly, first, upstream, the General Assembly and, downstream, with all existing organs dealing with human rights and the environment.

(i) Newly-defined areas of action for the Trusteeship Council: the rights of present and future generations

We will deal here, respectively, first with the Council's protection of the present generation's human rights and, then, with its promotion and taking into account of future generations' interests, that is, primarily, the preservation of the human environment, in the broadest possible sense.

The promotion of the present generation's human rights

First, let us recall that the first of the most fundamental human rights or, more precisely, the necessary prerequisite and the *sine qua non* condition for the full achievement of any other human right, is the realization of the right to self-determination, which is an attribute of all peoples. This is the meaning of the common Article 1 of the two Covenants on human rights of December 1966, which states (paragraph 1): 'All peoples have the right of self-determination. By virtue of that right they freely determine their political status and freely pursue their economic, social and cultural development.' This fundamental position explains why this right has been stated in the very first article of both Covenants; thus, the realization of this right determines both the achievement of civil and political rights, and the exercise of economic, social and cultural rights, that is, the whole range of human rights.[12] The new Trusteeship Council will therefore have to pursue its initial aim, that is, the achievement of full independence by peoples.

Indeed, it can be argued that there has appeared, since the end of the cold war and the end of the decolonization process, a new meaning and new dimensions to the right of all peoples to self-determination, even though this evolution has not entered *lex lata* yet, and is still part of *lex ferenda*;[13] in other words, it still has to be confirmed by practice. This evolution mainly concerns the numerous minorities and indigenous populations throughout the world, which endeavour to equate their own status with that

---

[12] Indeed, as most scholars agree today, the so-called 'third generation' of human rights – such as the right to peace, the right to economic development or the right to a healthy natural environment – does not encompass human (that is, individual) rights, but involves concepts which have a collective nature; they certainly have a link to human rights – to the extent that they can be seen as a prerequisite to their full achievement – but they should not be seen themselves as human rights. To that extent, it can be argued that the right to self-determination is itself such a 'third generation' right.

[13] *Lex lata* designates, when applied to general international law, the corpus of law or rights as it presently exists and is actually applied at a given moment, whereas *lex ferenda* identifies an area of international law not yet (or not totally and generally) accepted by most actors of international law, that is, mainly, States, but still in (trans)formation.

1. The UN Security Council recommends Malta unanimously to the General assembly

2. The then Prime Minister Dr G. Borg Olivier
delivering Malta's first statement to the General
Assembly on 2 December 1964

3. The first delegation of Malta to the United Nations General Assembly

4. Malta's first delegation to the UN General Assembly meeting with the then
    Secretary-General U Thant

5. 1920–Parade in Geneva preceeding the first session of the
Assembly of the League of Nations

6. 1920–First session of the Assembly of the League of Nations

7.   1920–Meeting of the Council of the League of Nations
(Palais Wilson, Geneva)

8.   1938–Council Room of the League of Nations, Palais des Nations, Geneva

9. The Palais Wilson in Geneva, recently destroyed by fire, served as the Headquarters of the League before the move to the Palais des Nations

10. Handing over the assets of the League of Nations to the United Nations

11. 1946–Banquet in honour of UN delegates in London given by King George VI

12. Security Council Chamber

13. Trusteeship Council Chamber

15. Professor Guido de Marco, President of the UN General Assembly forty-fifth
session, observing a moment of silence at the close of the session

which entitles peoples to self-determination.[14] Therefore, the new Trusteeship Council will have to scrutinize closely this evolution and, once it becomes part of *lex lata*, would have to play the same role as the one it performed during the process of decolonization, that is, organizing and accompanying the process, *mutatis mutandis*, so that it evolves as peacefully as possible.

As far as human rights as such are concerned, it should be noted that the extension of the Council's mandate to that area should not be a problem. At least two reasons – both grounded in the present Charter – allow us to make that assumption. First of all, human rights are already part of the Trusteeship Council's mandate. Indeed, Article 76(c) states: 'The basic objectives of the trusteeship system, in accordance with the Purposes of the United Nations laid down in Article 1 of the present Charter, shall be ... to encourage respect for human rights and fundamental freedoms for all without distinction as to race, sex, language, or religion, and to encourage recognition of the interdependence of the peoples of the world.'

Secondly, the Trusteeship Council itself is endowed by the Charter with all the instruments which are usually given, within the United Nations, to organs entrusted with the protection or promotion of human rights, that is, (annual) reports, petitions or 'communications', and the possibility to organize on-the-spot visits to the field, especially in cases of massive or systematic violations of human rights. Thus, Article 87 of the Charter states:

The General Assembly and, under its authority, the Trusteeship Council, in carrying out their functions, may:

a. consider reports submitted by the administering authority;

b. accept petitions and examine them in consultation with the administering authority;

c. provide for periodic visits to the respective trust territories at times agreed upon with the administering authority ...

Such machinery and procedures would be very useful, in particular, in cases of total breakdown of legal and political

---

[14] The example of the Kurds is relevant here. This case – strikingly exemplifying the conflict and present tension between the *lex lata* and the *lex ferenda* in the area of self-determination – is particularly significant but is also complicated by the fact that the Kurdish population is scattered across the national territory of three different States (Turkey, Iran and Iraq), and sometimes encounters hostile attitudes. But a new, revitalized Trusteeship Council – as envisaged and described here – would be particularly useful and vital for populations in similar situations.

institutions – whether or not accompanied by genocide or so-called 'ethnic cleansing'.

To return to the broader and more general case of human rights, we have no difficulty with the present Centre for Human Rights as recently restructured, which includes of course the Office of the High Commissioner for Human Rights. The basic difference we would propose would be that the Trusteeship Council rather than ECOSOC be responsible for the overall guidance and monitoring of United Nations work in this area. An added advantage to this idea is that ECOSOC would concentrate on its work as clearly mandated by the Charter. This will be developed in the next chapter.

The protection of future generations' well-being

The main contribution that the Trusteeship Council – or any other United Nations organ – can make is certainly the preservation of the human environment. This is now recognized as an objective of the United Nations. Though not alone in the consolidation of this trend, Malta's contribution to its promotion has been significant. In particular, Malta's role in 1967 in raising international awareness of a common heritage as applicable to the sea-bed, the ocean floor and the subsoil thereof underlying the high seas beyond the limits of national jurisdiction is now part of history. Twenty-one years later, during the forty-third session of the Assembly, Malta played a leading role in bringing to the fore what is probably the most serious environmental concern humanity has ever had to face – the problem of climate change. The adoption of General Assembly resolution 43/53 in December 1988, which characterized climate change as a common concern of mankind, focused world attention on this problem. A number of meetings world-wide followed this resolution, culminating in the Framework Convention on Climate Change.

In August 1989, Malta requested the inclusion in the provisional agenda of the forty-fourth session of the Assembly of a supplementary sub-item (under item 83) entitled 'Environmental protection of extra-territorial spaces for present and future generations.' The recommendation focused on the identification and extent of extra-territorial spaces, the rights and duties of States and the international community therein, the possible strengthening of relevant existing legal instruments, and the effective and comprehensive environmental protection of such spaces. A draft resolution was formally introduced in the Second Committee of the Assembly on 20 November 1989, after which it was examined in informal consultations in one of the working Groups of the Committee chaired by one of its Vice-Chairmen. In its decision 44–51, the General Assembly, on the recommendation of the Second Committee, decided to take no action on the draft resolution 'at the present time', thus leaving the door open for further consideration of the Maltese initiative.

However, the failure of the Assembly to adopt a text on this important subject was, fortunately enough, mitigated by an important development in the International Law Commission and in the Preparatory Committee for UNCED. Special Rapporteur, Professor Julio Barboza, in his sixth report deals extensively and in detail on the liability for harm to the environment in areas beyond national jurisdiction – that which Malta had described in its proposal to the United Nations as extra-territorial spaces. Yet another development was the text being considered for discussion in UNCED relating to the sustainable use and conservation of the high seas' living resources. It is, precisely, within this overall context of Malta's engagement in favour of the protection and the taking into account of our global commons that we have proposed the reform of the Trusteeship Council as the body most appropriate to act as trustee of the global commons in the interest of future generations.

Having analysed the new *ratione materiae* competence of the Council, we wish now to turn to the analysis of its newly defined functions in the United Nations institutional order, at least as we envision it.

(ii) Newly defined functions for the Trusteeship Council: implementation and coordination.

The first new function of the Council would be justified by Article 85(2) of the Charter, quoted above, but worth repeating here: 'The Trusteeship Council, operating under the authority of the General Assembly, shall assist the Assembly in carrying out (its) functions.' More precisely, we have described in chapter five how the Assembly should be reorganized and, specifically, we have stated that it should determine the general orientation and direction for all United Nations institutions, especially through summits and its 'regular annual session' (which would be made continuous) dealing with and being responsible for the follow-up and control of the implementation of its decisions. At this level – and in regard to what has just been said about its new competence – the Council would be entrusted with the application of the directions and orientations defined by the Assembly in the areas of 'common interest of mankind' and, in particular, in areas dealing with human rights and the human environment.

However, the Trusteeship Council itself would not be in charge of the implementation of these decisions *per se*; indeed, there already exists a full range of organs or agencies entrusted with various aspects of the protection of human rights or the environment. In the present situation, we do not believe that, realistically, these should or could be simply eliminated. Indeed, some of these organs do make a valuable contribution; in particular, the work of those aimed at controlling the application of universal human rights instruments such as the Human Rights Committee,[15] should be emphasized, however weak the protection provided may appear, especially when compared with some regional instruments such as the European Convention on Human Rights or its inter-American counterpart.

Moreover, if the existing United Nations machinery in the areas of human rights or human environment does not have optimum efficiency at the moment, it can be argued that this is mainly due to the lack of coordination between respective organs, each of them dealing with problems which are closely related and which constantly interact and intertwine, but each of them continuing to work in its own separate, well-defined area.

Thus, the principal role of the Trusteeship Council would be to coordinate and 'bond the linkage' between the various organs or agencies dealing with human rights and the human environment. In particular, it would have to coordinate United Nations activities not only in the area of human rights itself, of course, but also those conducted in the sphere of the environent. Indeed,

---

[15] Its role is to control the implementation of the Covenant on Civil and Political Rights, in particular through: 1. regular governmental reports, and 2. if the State has agreed by the ratification of a particular protocol to the Covenant, the possibility given to individuals who claim to be victims of violations of their civil or political human rights to submit 'communications' to the Committee. Both reports and decisions of the Committee being published – at least partly – these procedures can and do have an impact on the situation of human rights in the countries in question.

as already stated, respect for human rights does not make much sense in a country or in a world where people cannot breathe pure air or are threatened by the depletion of the ozone layer.

Therefore it is clear that the Trusteeship Council would be the major and central United Nations organ in the area of human rights and environment, and not merely an additional organ aimed at the protection of these two aspects of human life, domains in which several other secondary organs and agencies are already active. The Trusteeship Council would not even act as a kind of *primus inter pares* with them, but rather as a (hierarchically) superior, coordinating and supervisory body. Achieving coherence and better coordination would improve the credibility and the legitimacy of United Nations action in these spheres – especially that of human rights.

As far as the protection of the global human environment is concerned, we can identify at present a number of areas which are considered as part of a common heritage, and covered by conventions and General Assembly resolutions. Among them are the sea-bed and ocean floor, biodiversity, environment, climate, and outer space. These areas are entrusted to a number of distinct international institutions, amongst which are: the International Sea Authority; the Commission for Sustainable Development; the Inter-Governmental Panel on Climate Change; and the United Nations Environment Programme (UNEP). These institutions work independently, in an almost completely uncoordinated fashion. Though each aspect requires specific attention, the intrinsic linkage between the different issues demands a united effort. The concept of common heritage requires a coordinated approach. A change of one element affects the functioning of the whole. Interrelationships cannot be ignored. A scenario of institutional fragmentation can only be avoided through the establishment of an oversight mechanism relative to those areas held in trust for future generations.

A similar assessment may be made regarding human rights problems: but we will not dwell on this aspect. However, some interesting developments in this area should be noted and encouraged. In particular, as stated by Malta at the forty-eighth session of the Assembly: 'We consider the recent establishment of the International Tribunal for the Prosecution of Persons Responsible for Serious Violations of International Law committed in the Territory of the Former Yugoslavia as a pledge that the heinous crimes against humanity will not remain unpunished. However, we believe that the setting-up of an international criminal court, vested with jurisdiction to try crimes against humanity, war crimes, international terrorism and global traffic in narcotics would provide a framework corresponding to the international dimension of such offences.'[16]

More generally, the extremely valuable work of the International Law Commission should be closely followed and encouraged with the new Trusteeship Council's help and collaboration; indeed, besides the future establishment of an international criminal court, the Commission is studying other topics which are relevant to the work of the Trusteeship Council, namely those relevant to the protection of present and future generations. Thus, for example, the concept of common heritage, as applied to the human environment, is echoed in the work of the International Law Commission. Indeed, during the period when Malta was introducing this concept, some members of the Commission had acknowledged, during its 1991 session, that the problem of continuous deterioration of the human environment was a serious matter with universal implications which needed to be addressed by the International Law Commission and suggested that 'the Trusteeship Council's mandate could be changed and be extended to cover the protection of the resources of the global commons'.

Thus, efforts of the Commission to codify and further the progressive evolution of the international norms should be encouraged and welcomed, as today more than ever, it is apparent that the necessary precondition for a safer and saner world is a more lawful world order.

---

[16] *Op. cit.*, p. 8.

SEVEN

ECOSOC AND THE BRETTON WOODS INSTITUTIONS: NEW ECONOMIC AND SOCIAL STRUCTURES

Summary

While the responsibilities assigned by the Charter to ECOSOC – 'the creation of conditions of stability and well-being which are necessary for peaceful and friendly relations among nations'[1] – were certainly awe-inspiring, the fact is that the Council did not live up to them and fell short of the expectations of Member States. ECOSOC was almost immediately pre-empted by other organizations, especially the Bretton Woods organizations, and, as a result, the first fifty years saw ECOSOC rendered effectively impotent, never to produce the desired results. We believe that it is time to return to the original principles and intentions for ECOSOC, revitalizing and strengthening its mandate in international economic and social affairs, emphasizing its leading role and the complementarity of the other economic and social institutions, including, primarily, the Bretton Woods institutions. This will not be easy. This is an area where North-South entrenched positions have not moved an iota in the last 50 years and it is not realistic to expect any miracles in this respect in the future. We feel, however, that our proposals may offer possibilities for breaking the deadlock.

(a) *ECOSOC's Role*

Although the Economic and Social Council (ECOSOC) was intended to complement the work of the Security Council and

---

[1] Chapter IX, Article 55.

work towards the cultivation of peace by coordinating international economic and social cooperation, it has failed to fulfil its mandate, as outlined by the Charter, to promote:

a. higher standards of living, full employment, and conditions of economic and social progress and development;

b. solutions of international economic, social, health, and related problems; and international cultural and educational cooperation; and

c. universal respect for, and observance of, human rights and fundamental freedoms for all without distinction as to race, sex, language, or religion.[2]

Was it realistic to expect ECOSOC to carry such heavy responsibilities in the areas of economics, social affairs and human rights? We think not – at least not in the way ECOSOC developed. In our opinion, this was, and still is, a classic case of a body with enormous responsibilities but without the necessary authority to be able to act decisively.

In the economic and social areas, but particularly in the economic, ECOSOC and the United Nations never exercised the kind of leadership that was stipulated in the Charter. In this regard the United Nations was relegated, from the beginning, to the status of observer and as such, it followed the leadership of the Bretton Woods institutions (primarily the World Bank and the International Monetary Fund). The Bretton Woods institutions, established a few months before the United Nations, have dictated virtually all international economic and financial matters in the post-Second World War period. ECOSOC never fulfilled the vision set out in the Charter of overseeing the international economy. Instead, the World Bank quickly became the focal point for, *inter alia*, development loans, while the IMF emerged as the key actor helping countries out of balance-of-payments problems. Moreover, the Bank and the Fund, because of the strict conditions attached to their loans, often exercised an enormous amount of power over weaker developing countries, while developed countries escaped any sanction for errant policies. For example, IMF, in its *World Economic Outlook*, repeatedly called on countries such as the United States in the 1980s and 1990s to reduce their severe budget and current account deficits in order, *inter alia*, to alleviate pressures on global interest rates.

---

[2] *Ibid.*

However, unlike in the case of developing countries, the IMF was effectively powerless to impose such policy prescriptions and the calls went largely unheeded.

As a result, ECOSOC and the United Nations never played an important role in these areas, except, perhaps, in the field of analytical work and research, yet even there they often duplicated work undertaken by the Bretton Woods institutions, such as surveys of the international economy and predictions of economic prospects. This is a clear example of the duplication problem that is analysed in chapter eight.

In this chapter, which deals mainly with economic and social aspects of the work, we shall try to identify the reasons for the failure of ECOSOC and attempt to reorient the on-going debate. There can be no true peace without equitable development and ECOSOC must be reinvigorated to play a central role in this process. In order to allow ECOSOC to specialize in these development issues, our proposals will include transferring treatment of human rights to the Trusteeship Council. This is in line with Malta's initiative to transform the Trusteeship Council into a major organ of the Second Generation United Nations to safeguard the rights of future generations and the rights of people whose human rights are not respected.

The hectic pace of the most recent phase of restructuring of the economic and social sectors of the United Nations and the streamlining of ECOSOC should be seen in the context of the limited impact the United Nations has had in economic and social matters. The ongoing restructuring of the economic and social sectors should equip the United Nations to enable it to make a significant and lasting contribution to economic and social development, particularly of the less developed countries. A crucial element in all this is a changed relationship between the United Nations (and its agencies) and the Bretton Woods institutions.

In this new relationship the logic of development employed by the Bretton Woods institutions must come closer to the logic of development of developing countries and not the other way around. Token gestures, such as attending each other's meetings, can no longer suffice. Bold action will be needed to implement this new, clearer and more transparent relationship – perhaps the equivalent in the North-South relationship of the East-West détente. This is what we should aim for.

(b) *The Bretton Woods Agreement*

The Bretton Woods agreement in 1944 laid the framework for the present international economic order, and the World Bank and the IMF were two institutions that came out of this agreement. The main concern of developed countries at Bretton Woods was the reconstruction of Europe and the world economy. Another concern was the slow economic growth that would have resulted if they could not find export markets for their products. Trade was governed substantially by the theory of international trade and finance based on the principle of comparative advantage. As a result, the economies of developing countries, most of them suppliers of raw materials, depended very heavily on the economic policies of the developed, industrialized countries.

This situation drew attention to the economic development of developing countries and encouraged a great development debate that led the United Nations to give greater importance and emphasis to the economic and social aspects of its work. The international development strategy of the 1960s was supposed to assist developing countries to attain their 'take-off' for sustainable growth and development. The international development strategy of this first development decade was a failure and fell below the expectations of many in the developing world. The second development decade followed, more or less, in the footsteps of the first. The decades, strategies, special sessions and the United Nations meetings which followed did not result in anything concrete. The developing countries increasingly realized that, without changes in the world economic order, they were destined to continue playing a secondary role, with their economic development dictated by, and dependent upon, the developed countries.

That the Bretton Woods logic of development was not, and is still not, the logic of development of the developing countries is demonstrated by the fact that the World Bank did not consider loans for agricultural development until Robert McNamara's presidency. (A primary objective of not giving loans for agriculture was to ensure the dependency of the developing countries on agricultural imports from the United States.) The Bretton Woods institutions promoted international specialization of production along the lines dictated by 'comparative advantage' despite increasing indications in economic literature that this was not in the interest of the weaker of the partners (namely the developing countries) in international trade.[3]

Thus it becomes clear that proposals for the United Nations to attend World Bank and IMF meetings are insufficient. This would prove as ineffective as Bretton Woods representatives attending United Nations meetings (which they have been doing for some time). They diligently attend meetings and thoughtfully participate in debates but when it comes to taking decisions or passing resolutions, they respectfully 'abstain' or 'absent themselves' and explain that: '. . . the General Assembly has no authority over the Bretton Woods institutions'. It is clear that attempts at friendly persuasion in this respect (such as General Assembly resolutions which 'recommend to Bretton Woods . . .') have not worked and may never work.

(c) *SUNFED to UNDP*

This unhappiness with the Bretton Woods institutions is not new. During the development debate at the United Nations in the 1950s, the developing countries obliged the General Assembly to establish SUNFED – the Special United Nations Fund for Economic Development. This apparent victory for the developing countries and the United Nations was short-lived. The donor countries did not contribute to it and, moreover, the International Development Association (IDA) was established within the World Bank as an alternative to SUNFED. By placing the IDA within the Bretton Woods system, developed countries ensured that it would be governed by regulations and procedures such as the weighted voting system that centralizes power in their hands. Attempts by the United Nations to forge a closer relationship between itself and the IDA failed.[4] Another development was the establishment of the United Nations Development Programme (UNDP), formed through the merger in 1965 of two United Nations technical assistance programmes (the Expanded Programme of Technical Assistance of 1949 and the Special Fund of 1959). It was through UNDP, which reported to ECOSOC,

---

[3] See, for example, Raul Prebisch, *Towards a Global Strategy of Development*, United Nations, New York, 1968; Hans Singer, *International Development: Growth and Change*, McGraw-Hill, New York, 1964.
[4] Sydney Dell, 'Relations between the United Nations and the Bretton Woods Institutions', in *Development*, 1989:4, SID, Rome.

that the United Nations hoped to exercise its authority over development and technical assistance.[5]

The aborted attempt to establish SUNFED represented the last time that the United Nations made a serious effort to solve the problem of its relationship with the World Bank and the IMF. It was also the last time that developing countries tried to establish a multilateral source of capital assistance outside the Bretton Woods institutions.

(d) *The World Bank and IMF*

The Bretton Woods institutions have strayed from their original aims and increasingly have been charged with trying to control the domestic policies of developing countries, while being powerless to influence policies of developed countries.[6] Since the early 1980s, the World Bank and the IMF have been focused on ensuring that indebted developing countries are able to service their debt payments. This has meant the imposition, by means of conditionality, of stringent stabilization and structural adjustment policies which have resulted in lower standards of living and levels of investment that retard future growth and development prospects.

This institutional behaviour differs from the proposals outlined during discussions in the early 1940s, primarily between the United Kingdom and the United States, of the post-war international economic institutions. There were two competing visions regarding the post-war order, one outlined by the United States Treasury official Harry Dexter White (known as the White Plan), and the other by the British official John Maynard Keynes (the Keynes Plan).[7] Both plans (a synthesis of which led to the creation of IMF) were designed to facilitate the achievement of a balance-of-payments equilibrium in an environment of multilateral trade and in domestic conditions of full employment.

---

[5] For more on the United Nations' disappointing early experience with technical assistance, see Michael Bartolo, *Limitations of U.N. Technical Assistance*, ENDA document 5, Dakar, Senegal.

[6] See, for example, such early works as Teresa Hayter, *Aid as Imperialism*, New York: Penguin Books, 1971 and Cheryl Payer, *The Debt Trap: The IMF and the Third World*, New York: Penguin Books, 1974.

[7] For a review of the planning of the post-war international economic order, see Richard Gardner, *Sterling-Dollar Diplomacy in Current Perspective*, New York: Columbia University Press, 1980.

Both plans addressed disturbances to economic equilibrium of a short-term nature. The White Plan, however, stressed the problem of monetary stabilization, especially in the face of wide currency fluctuations, the speculative capital movements and the bank failures that plagued the world after the First World War. The Keynes Plan, on the other hand, proposed a Clearing Union that would make large overdraft facilities available to its members in order to ensure domestic expansion and guard against deflation and unemployment. Both plans envisaged a global environment characterized by a new world political order, free from the problems associated with the need for special alliances and traditional power politics.

The World Bank came about around the same time and was to address the concerns of the post-war planners to help countries to reconstruct their productive capacities and give them access to long-term capital assistance. The initial proposal was for a bold and ambitious Bank, well-financed and willing to involve itself in a wide degree of activities. By the time of the Bretton Woods Conference, the Bank had been scaled back significantly and turned into a conservative lending institution. This was largely due to American concerns that the Bank should primarily be concerned with aiding and encouraging the provision of private funds for international investment by means of guarantees, an aim that the new Bank president, James Wolfensohn, has reiterated upon his nomination.

At the same time as the Bretton Woods institutions began to diverge substantially from the United Nations in terms of economic development policies, the staff policies and systems also began to differ. Governments actively supported the increase in the Bretton Woods staff while simultaneously demanding United Nations staff reductions. For example, the World Bank's professional-level staff doubled between 1979 and 1992 while the United Nations was forced to cut its staff by 13 per cent.[8] Moreover, the pay scales of the Bretton Woods institutions have become significantly higher than those in the United Nations. For example, World Bank Group professionals received around 35 per cent more than their counterparts in the United Nations Secretariat.[9] This has helped lead to the demoralization of more United Nations staff and has made it difficult for the United

[8] Childers and Urquhart, *op cit.*, p. 164.
[9] *Ibid.*, p 164.

91

Nations to attract top economists, sociologists, and other professionals.

(e) *Specialized Agencies of the United Nations*

As well as these economic shortcomings and their unusual evolution, the Bretton Woods institutions also suffer from a democracy deficit. Unlike at the United Nations, decisions at the World Bank and the IMF are not taken on the basis of one country, one vote, but on the basis of a system of weighted voting depending mainly on the country's contribution to the organizations. Moreover, the 'standard' specialized agency agreement with the United Nations signed by the Bretton Woods institutions differs from those of other specialized agencies, like FAO, ILO and others.[10] Bretton Woods institutions are not obliged to follow either the decisions taken by the General Assembly or other United Nations common system characteristics (such as the staff regulations). We believe that this is the crux of the matter and that unless this is changed, the United Nations will never play a significant role in international economic (and social) matters.

How can an East-West détente in the North-South relationship come about? What would be the United Nations role? As unrealistic as it would appear at present, the only effective and just solution to this problem would be to give the General Assembly, especially through a revitalized ECOSOC, some kind of authority over the Bretton Woods institutions. This could be achieved by returning to the principles outlined originally in the Charter: the General Assembly should lay down the main goals and outlines that promote international economic and social co-operation and the ECOSOC should ensure that all agencies within the greater United Nations system are working towards the effective implementation of these goals. In more practical terms, this would mean that ECOSOC would be involved in the elaboration of World Bank and IMF policies and, where these clash with General Assembly decisions, ensure that the Bretton Woods institutions are obliged to change their practices and harmonize them with General Assembly guidelines. This could only come about by democratizing the World Bank and the IMF. We know, however, that there will be no perestroika without glasnost.

[10] Robert E. Asher and Edward S. Masin, *The World Bank since Bretton Woods*, 1973, p 58.

In the present circumstances, very little can be achieved from the restructuring of the economic and social sectors of the United Nations. There is no doubt that duplication and waste can be eliminated and that the United Nations can be made more efficient in these areas. Reform proposals such as the *Agenda for Development* and others may be good starts, but they do not go far enough. As stated with regard to the work of the General Assembly, efficiency without relevance is a step backward. There is no point in raising expectations unless the political will exists to put the Bretton Woods institutions under the authority of the General Assembly. Admittedly, this is not an easy task and should not be expected to come about during the 50th Anniversary of the United Nations or soon thereafter.

The United Nations recently obliged the Bretton Woods institutions to put a 'human face' on the logic of their development. Now the time has come for the United Nations to oblige Member States to introduce frankness and transparency into the debate on the relationship between the United Nations and the World Bank and IMF. How this can be done should now be the paramount concern of the United Nations.

(f) *Reforming the Bretton Woods Institutions*

There have been many suggestions for reform of the Bretton Woods institutions and proposals to improve their working relationship with the United Nations but most of these proposals are not bold enough to face the development challenges of the twenty-first century. For example, the Secretary-General has put forward in the *Agenda for Development* many sound recommendations for strengthening the role of ECOSOC and improving cooperation between the United Nations and the Bretton Woods institutions. The *Agenda* calls on the Bretton Woods institutions to strengthen their links with the United Nations by increasing cooperation and collaboration on a wide range of issues and on specific programmes. Moreover, the Secretary-General suggests reactivating the United Nations/Bretton Woods liaison committee to improve communication and play an active role in the Bank/Fund Development Committee's deliberations. However, these proposals would leave the present situation, and the autonomous nature of the Bretton Woods institutions, largely intact and therefore not bring the desired results any closer.

Similarly, the World Bank and IMF have been considering their own internal reforms. Some, like those proposed by Michel Camdessus, Managing Director of IMF, involve a number of interesting suggestions, including emphasizing 'high-quality growth' by expanding the scope of IMF beyond balances of payments to include such vital concerns as poverty and the environment. Also, an increase in the allocation of Special Drawing Rights (SDRs) to improve the development prospects of developing countries should be welcomed by all. The World Bank has also endeavoured to review its priorities and improve its effectiveness by streamlining its operations and orienting its work to each client's specific needs. Moreover, the new Bank president, James Wolfensohn, has outlined his visions for the future that include further encouragement of private investment and reducing the Bank's activities in technical cooperation. However, these proposals largely ignore the role of the United Nations and would preclude any incursion into the Bank's autonomy.

(g) Reforming ECOSOC

A provocative suggestion has come from the Commission on Global Governance. In its report, entitled *Our Global Neighbourhood*, it proposes to abolish ECOSOC and replace it with an Economic Security Council that would have more and wider-ranging powers. However, given the political will, ECOSOC could be reformed to carry out all the functions proposed for the Economic Security Council. This could be achieved by a General Assembly summit at the highest political level encouraging world leaders to speak with a single voice that could not be ignored. Moreover, this proposal would avoid the difficult and cumbersome task of substantially modifying the Charter – a Charter that we believe already contains all the essential elements of an effective system of global governance.

Another set of proposals has come from the Nordic Under-Secretaries-General for International Development Cooperation who delivered their final report to the General Assembly in 1991 (A/C.2/46/7). The Nordic Initiative tried to establish a clear division of roles and mandates between the General Assembly and ECOSOC and set up small executive bodies for each United Nations fund and programme. These proposals included suggestions to fuse the Second and Third Committees of the General Assembly or to abolish them and strengthen and enlarge ECOSOC in order to transform it into a universal body meeting in parallel with the General Assembly. While the initiative foundered, it does contain some interesting elements for discussion, and in fact comes closest to our own proposals.

A developing trend is seen in the nascent discussions between the World Bank, IMF and the newly established World Trade Organization (WTO). In WTO's call for 'coherence' in global economic policy-making, it proposes new formal links between these three organizations. This should be encouraged but care must be taken to avoid the creation of a network that may effectively side-step the United Nations and create a parallel and competing institutional decision-making structure. This should be avoided or brought under the revitalized ECOSOC through discussions that should take place regularly between the heads of United Nations and specialized agencies and ECOSOC. Still, at this point, with WTO continuing to fashion its own niche in the realm of international economic institutions, it may be too early to impose constraints on it. WTO is moving in a fruitful and constructive direction and it may be unfair to force it to align itself too closely with the United Nations until United Nations reforms are completed.

The World Summit on Social Development in March 1995 also signalled some emerging trends. It was clear to most delegates that poverty and social dislocations around the world have global consequences, such as severe migration patterns, health epidemics and economies too risky and poor for investors and exporters. There was much support for the Group of 77's proposal for donor countries and institutions to earmark 20 per cent of their foreign aid to basic social needs, to be matched by developing countries committing 20 per cent of their own expenditures to the same underfinanced sectors. However, there were also signs from developed countries of a growing weariness to fund programmes that are popularly considered ineffective. Indeed, United States Vice-President Al Gore announced that within five years, the United States will channel half of its foreign aid through private organizations and not through governments.

Clearly, then, the area of development assistance is changing significantly. In the past, UNDP was charged with coordinating this development assistance, but we believe that the time has come for governments to rethink the role and purpose of UNDP. We propose that the United Nations and the Bretton Woods institutions converge, which would imply a serious re-evaluation of such an institution as UNDP. As a result, we call on governments to analyse UNDP seriously in order to determine whether the original aims and goals are still relevant today.

(h) *New United Nations Economic and Social Structures*

The proposals for reform by various authors outlined above, fall short, we believe, of a comprehensive and equitable treatment of the economic and social challenges that will face the world in the twenty-first century. We believe that a return to the principles and concepts outlined in the Charter can best equip the United Nations to overcome such challenges. With this in mind, we propose the following:

a. Heads of State or Government should, during one of the earliest United Nations General Assembly summits, affirm their commitment to revitalize ECOSOC by allowing it to perform the global economic security functions that were envisioned in the Charter.

b. The structure and procedures of ECOSOC should be modified in order to facilitate improved policy dialogue. This should include the involvement of ministers in the work of ECOSOC, making the high-level ministerial session of ECOSOC a regular annual feature. Sessions at the Heads of State or Government level, to maintain the political impetus needed to perform effectively, should coincide with the decennial General Assembly summits.

c. Better coordination and cooperation between international economic and social bodies must be pursued effectively. All mandates and programmes must be reviewed with the aim of eliminating duplication – even if this means the down-sizing or elimination of some agencies. The mandate of UNDP, in particular, must be reviewed since the above proposals for the harmonization of the United Nations and the Bretton Woods institutions may leave little place for UNDP as it functions at present.

d. The Bretton Woods institutions need to be reformed and some degree of authority over their policies and goals should be accorded the General Assembly and ECOSOC. IMF and the

World Bank need to be democratized and strengthened so as to be able to address threats to macroeconomic stability and development – whether these threats originate in developed or developing countries. Their mandates must be considered in a broader perspective to view development as a holistic and multi-faceted process that includes social as well as economic aspects. The World Bank should not reduce its activities in the area of technical cooperation. In fact, our proposals for a Second Generation United Nations see the Bank increasing its role in this regard to facilitate closer cooperation with the United Nations in the policy area. In the area of technical cooperation, the Bank would be assisted by the strengthened United Nations Regional Commissions, the Regional Banks and the United Nations specialized agencies.

e. The relationship between the General Assembly and ECOSOC needs to be strengthened and the main feature of this strengthening may involve the transfer of responsibilities from the Second and Third Committees, the granting of more authority to ECOSOC and direct links with the General Assembly decennial summit.

f. The above should proceed in the larger context of the United Nations system restructuring which may include more decentralization of economic and social operational work to the Bretton Woods institutions. In fact, the United Nations Secretariat should not be involved in any technical cooperation activities at all, except in the context of the necessary preparations for sessions of ECOSOC and that of strengthening the Regional Economic Commissions.

g. The streamlined specialized agencies would again become major partners, as associates in the area of assistance to developing countries.

h. The time-frame for these reforms would be decided by ECOSOC and the Bretton Woods institutions.

i. Regarding staff quality, such a major overhaul in the Economic and Social System of the United Nations must also consider the present human resources in both the United Nations and the Bretton Woods institutions (which tend to be of higher quality). Attempts should be made to reform and harmonize staff policies with the aim of establishing a single staff system.

Why do we believe that such a scenario could realistically be acceptable to all Member States? First, our proposals are related directly to the role and mandate for ECOSOC, as outlined originally in the Charter, to act as the lead organization in the United Nations system, laying down the broad guidelines and giving the whole system clear policy directions. Secondly, we propose a new and more ambitious role for the Bretton Woods institutions that would allow them to consolidate their autonomy, while following ECOSOC's broad guidelines. The Bretton Woods institutions would take over operational activities in their fields and implement policies with the close cooperation of specialized agencies. However, they would maintain the major role assigned to them by the Bretton Woods Conference. We believe that these proposals should not overly worry countries, especially larger, developed countries, since all the work of the United Nations and related institutions would be carried out in the context of the Summit of the General Assembly, which would act as the highest oversight body in the Second Generation United Nations.

31. Our proposals for a Second Generation System of Economic Institutions of the United Nations are set out in diagram 2.

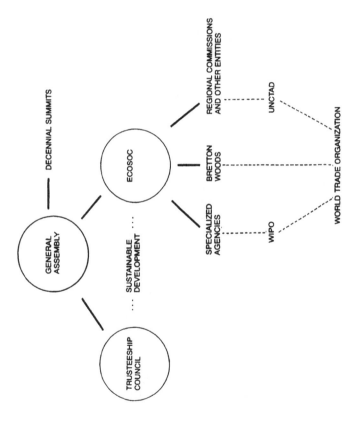

Diagram 2: **Second Generation Economic and Social Institutions of the United Nations**

EIGHT

STREAMLINING BY ELIMINATING OVERLAPPING AND BY ENSURING BETTER COORDINATION

Summary

This chapter as compared with the others is inevitably more politically sensitive for it tackles the most difficult challenge that any institution may face: the elimination of existing organs, which may be vigorously opposed from within and from the outside. Yet pruning is necessary if we wish to make the United Nations an effective and relevant system. Coordination, more politically feasible, is also essential and sometimes implies major restructuring. Nevertheless, no endeavour for reform can be meaningful without the participation and the support of Member States. Moreover, coordination in the United Nations system is also a reflection of coordination of the policies of the various Governments. This problem should not be underestimated and the blame for failure in this regard should not be placed solely on the United Nations. Governments also need to play their part. This chapter will try to set the trend by giving practical examples of realignment in some of the major areas of the United Nations.

(a) *Leaner and More Transparent*

It is impossible in a study of this kind to be comprehensive – we are therefore obliged to be selective – but with enough examples to show a rational and unmistakable trend towards a leaner and more transparent organization.

Politically this is not an easy chapter – as we have seen by the reaction of regional groups to recent proposals to eliminate

100

UNCTAD and UNIDO. We shall try to be more selective and will only propose eliminating entities and organs when absolutely necessary. In the final analysis it is up to the majority of Member States to decide on the outcome of proposals for change in the United Nations system, whether such proposals come from within the United Nations or from the outside.

Malta is still a member of the Non-Aligned Movement (NAM) as currently defined and still participates in meetings of the Group of 77 which is, in a sense, the economic and social arm of NAM. However, Malta is now clearly on the threshold of European Union membership. This unique perspective permits us to appreciate the positions of the various regional groupings and therefore to present a point of view which may be more widely acceptable.

However, we wish to emphasize that even if all the above-mentioned reform proposals were implemented, they would certainly not be sufficient to render the United Nations more efficient and more relevant to present international problems and concerns. Indeed, in order to reach that goal, the proposals made in previous chapters, will have to be accompanied by an improved coordination throughout the United Nations system.

Governments have increasingly blamed the United Nations system for its lack of coordination. It seems that this criticism reflects two problems in one: the United Nations system is too unwieldy to be coordinated and Governments are themselves unable to coordinate their own policies, thereby making the problem of coordination probably unsolvable. Clearly, coordination at the inter-governmental level could work rather well if Governments gave it more importance. The Committee for Programme Coordination, for example, would be more effective if Governments granted it more importance and nominated more senior level representatives to serve on it.

Among other reasons, '(t)he acceptance of the autonomy of the specialized agencies and the frailty of ECOSOC have led to the chronic problems of the multiplication of organs, their overlapping of functions and failure to co-ordinate their programmes. The kind of authoritative leadership displayed by the Security Council in assisting the diminution of conflict in the late 1980s needs to be paralleled in the economic-social and environment spheres. Although this confusion has occasioned frequent and bitter complaints, the will for the radical institutional reform that is required seems utterly lacking.'[1] It is, precisely, that political will that we would like to spark off or, at least to encourage, by the following proposals to eliminate some of the most common and inadmissible overlapping or competitive functions between existing United Nations organs or agencies that handicap the whole entity, and plague its credibility in the eyes of both Member States and international public opinion.

To regain the necessary credibility and support from the Member States two steps should be taken: first of all, some existing organs or agencies should be reformed or discontinued; and, secondly, once the first operation has been completed, effective coordination and collaboration should be instituted between those United Nations organs or agencies that remain.

(b) *Reform of Existing Organs*

The United Nations should strive for a system-wide approach to world problems, especially in the areas of humanitarian affairs, and sustainable economic and social development. Moreover, there can be no peace without development, for economic and social measures are intrinsically linked to the political environment of a country and, thus, to the general security of any particular region and must therefore be thoroughly integrated and no longer regarded separately.

There is an evident need for the survival and strengthening of the whole United Nations system. Since 1945, the United Nations machinery, which was rather straightforward at first, has evolved in a very complicated manner and, more importantly, into an incredibly complex system of subsidiary organs, committees, sub-committees, commissions and other entities. Indeed, the Charter provided, for most of the 'principal organs' it instituted, 'to establish such organs as (they) deem necessary for the performance of (their) functions.'[2] As time went by, these organs in turn either divided or created sub-organs, and so the process continued. The Organization now resembles a huge tree – hence

---

[1] Luard, *supra*, p. 184.
[2] For the General Assembly, see Art. 22; for the Security Council: Art. 29; ECOSOC: Art. 68, etc.

the necessity, after 50 years of institutional proliferation, for some judicious pruning.[3]

The process of institutional proliferation sometimes leads the numerous committees, sub-organs and commissions to even forget the initial goal for which they were created; and, ultimately puts the whole Organization at risk.

What follows is in no case an exhaustive list of United Nations organs or agencies to be reformed but should be taken as representative of those which should be either discontinued or refocused. Indeed, instead of reviewing the whole range of United Nations activities in virtually all spheres of economic, social, cultural, human or political interest – we shall take only a few cases which we believe to be characteristic. An analysis of all the major United Nations organs in these areas indicates that some of them should be either reformed, or simply eliminated – although the latter solution should not be the general rule but the exception.

Almost from the inception of the Organization, pressures began to build up for the establishment of active programmes in the economic field. Developing countries among the membership began to demand programmes of assistance for poorer countries. In 1948 the first very small step was taken in this direction: the establishment of a small programme of technical assistance, financed out of the regular budget. The developed countries, however, were totally opposed to financing aid out of their assessed contributions to the Organization. A year or two later, therefore, in the Extended Programme of Technical Assistance (EPTA), the principle was adopted of asking for voluntary contributions by Governments. Throughout the 1950s, the developing countries sought the establishment of a Special United Nations Fund for Economic Development (SUNFED). However, once again, the developed countries objected to any fund based on

---

[3] Some authors still tend to think, apparently, that the proliferation of subsidiary organs or committees remains a good thing in itself; Maurice Bertrand – although 'revolutionary' and radical in some of his much-repeated proposals for United Nations reform – seems to be one of these when he states: 'la prolifération des comités n'est pas un mal en soi: le nombre et la complexité des problèmes à traiter exigent qui'il y ait de nombreux lieux de rencontres et de discussion' (*L'ONU*, *op. cit.* p. 65). However, as we have already said, the United Nations should not simply be a huge international talking shop, where 'meeting' and 'discussion' become ultimate goals in themselves, and where oral participation and debate become more important than the logical end of that discussion, that is, the taking of decisions – effective and binding decisions.

the principle of assessed contributions or which duplicated funds available from other sources, including the Bretton Woods institutions. In 1958 they secured instead the establishment of a 'Special Fund', financed by voluntary contributions, which financed pre-investment programmes to survey and prepare for large-scale capital projects; an undertaking far more acceptable to the developed countries. The Special Fund was eventually merged in 1965 with the United Nations Technical Assistance Programme to establish the United Nations Development Programme (UNDP).

At this stage of the process one pertinent observation may already be made: the movement of institutional expansion often originates in an initiative taken by one Member State or, more often, a group of Member States – in this case, developing countries. Thus, in the area of development at least, the phenomenon of institutional outgrowth was symptomatic of a sense of deep frustration on the part of developing countries when confronted with the indifference of developed States. It follows that they attempted to attract the interest of developed countries by creating multiple organs in the expectation that this would result in additional resources for development.

Once such a movement has been launched, the internal dynamics of the Organization lead it to continue indefinitely, even if the initial need or preoccupation has vanished. In such a case the United Nations should reform itself by discontinuing the obsolete organ(s), but practice shows that the Organization is unable and/or unwilling to do so. Thus, if the initial responsibility for institutional inflation lies with Member States' initiatives, the responsibility for the continuance of the situation is a direct result of the Organization's unwillingness to discontinue marginal activities.

As pointed out in chapter seven, UNDP was established as a voluntary programme for development activities, mainly of a technical assistance nature. Most of its funds are raised in an annual pledging conference, during which Governments announce what they can provide for the following year. Today, one role which seems to justify the maintenance of UNDP is its distribution of funds among its executing agents (including specialized agencies of the United Nations) dealing with economic development. In fact, it can be argued that, from the beginning, UNDP was set up mainly as a result of efforts by developing countries to obtain additional funds for technical co-operation activities. We consider UNDP to be a prime candidate for reappraisal. Its major role of finding the most appropriate executing or implementing agency for country projects no longer exists. The General Assembly decided years ago that Govern-ments themselves should execute and implement their own projects. The additional resources that UNDP was supposed to generate did not materialize. In fact, the overall percentage of Overseas Development Assistance (ODA) that is channelled through UNDP may be too small to justify the costs and mainten-ance of such an Organization: in 1993, UNDP contributions for operational activities amounted to US$ 1.4 billion,[4] which repre-sented 2.5 per cent of total net official development assistance.[5]

However, if the time for this move has not yet come, our suggestion would be that UNDP not be involved in areas where specialized agencies already intervene. Thus, it should offer only policy guidance, continue to maintain a field presence and con-tinue to serve as a main funding agency, thereby being able to continue to reduce significantly its Headquarters staff. This reappraisal should also include its Office of Project Services (OPS) since, from its inception, this Office has been considered by some specialized agencies of the United Nations to be duplica-ting their operational activities. On the other hand, such reappraisal need not include the United Nations Volunteers (UNV) whose activities are widely appreciated and considered to be cost-effective.

In 1964 the United Nations was launched on another venture in the economic field. Once again, pressures had built up among developing countries for an organ that would be concerned specifically with the development and trade problems of poorer countries. This led to a regular series of Conferences and to a board and secretariat being established. The United Nations Conference on Trade and Development (UNCTAD), which is now a permanent organization, is headed by a Secretary-General appointed by the General Assembly on the recommendation of the Secretary-General of the United Nations. Despite some

---

[4] *Comprehensive Statistical Data on Operational Activities for Development for the Year 1993*, A/50/202/Add.2, 30 May 1995, p. 10.
[5] *Geographical Distribution of Financial Flows to Aid Recipients*, DAC-OECD, 1995, p. 216.

important UNCTAD achievements,[6] proposals to eliminate the organ have been put forward. We believe that in the last resort, the outcome should depend on UNCTAD itself: indeed, the institution has to prove that there is a 'niche' for it in the new United Nations (economic and financial) order. UNCTAD now has a unique opportunity to justify its continuation in the context of the newly established World Trade Organization (WTO). It could furnish WTO with a direct link to the United Nations by carrying out some of the research and pre-negotiation activities which could be done more efficiently by UNCTAD than by WTO itself. Two major events, namely the appointment of a new Secretary-General of UNCTAD intent on reform and the convening of a conference (UNCTAD IX, in May 1996) focused on redefining its direction, seem to have put UNCTAD on the right track.

The very same advice could be offered to the United Nations Industrial Development Organization (UNIDO), which some quarters similarly proposed for elimination. UNIDO also had its origins in developments within the United Nations of the 1950s referred to above. In fact, it is one of the most recent specialized agencies.[7] In its case, as in UNCTAD's, the necessary precondition for it to be maintained should be its internal re-thinking to redefine its *raison d'être* in view of the several other existing United Nations organs dealing with the same topic. We have always supported the objectives and work of UNIDO and continue to do so even at present. We believe, however, that UNIDO's best defence against calls for its elimination is to make a final effort at streamlining and at specializing in those few areas, agreed upon by the Member States, that most need its assistance. Only this way can there be a useful future for UNIDO in the Second Generation United Nations.

The United Nations promotes a great deal of discussion at the intergovernmental level on economic and developmental matters. The Second Committee of the Assembly also regularly discusses such questions, as well as the Third Committee – even though it is supposedly concerned exclusively with social, humanitarian and cultural matters. A large number of *ad hoc*

[6] Probably UNCTAD's single most important achievement is the scheme for a generalized system of preferences for developing countries, under which these receive more favoured treatment than rich countries for trade purposes in most of the markets of the developed States, without having to give reciprocal privileges in turn.

[7] UNIDO became an autonomous specialized agency in 1986.

conferences are arranged. Several commissions, committees and sub-committees, some of them permanent, meet in New York, Geneva and elsewhere to examine a particular topic, or to discuss particular agreements.

Overall, it appears that too many organs have emerged in the area of economic development – but the same could be said of many other spheres of United Nations action. Thus, even though such a radical solution as elimination is still difficult to contemplate, we believe that if these organs cannot find a new identity and a renewed *raison d'être* in the constantly evolving United Nations institutional environment, recourse will ultimately have to be had to that solution.

It is a question of survival, not only for the whole United Nations system but also, as far as the special question of economic development is concerned, for the well-being of developing countries. It is in no-one's interest that marginal activities continue within the United Nations system.

(c) *Coordination*

Two goals which are certainly not incompatible but, on the contrary, are complementary have to be taken into account here: first, the rational division of work aimed at avoiding overlapping, implying a reorganization of activities within the Organization; and secondly, a new, close collaboration in areas of common interest among United Nations organs. While the first point implies internal reorganization, the second involves a heightened coordination of all components of the United Nations system.

Specialization is a necessary condition to avoid overlapping. As stated above, each United Nations organ – once the whole institution has been reformed – should be entrusted with a precise mission. Each organ should concentrate on those matters it manages the best, in areas where it has acquired the most expertise.

(d) *Streamlining*

It is necessary therefore to undertake a reorganization of responsibilities within the United Nations. This implies the introduction of a much more hierarchical and authoritative structure within the Organization, the upper rung of the ladder being able to check on the one below it, and so on. Thus, the principle would be applied to the whole United Nations, from the top – the Assembly – to the bottom. We would emphasize that this is perfectly compatible with our proposal to place, for instance, all specialized economic, social and financial institutions under the authority of the Assembly, these institutions covering a wide variety of work that should be coordinated on behalf of the Assembly by ECOSOC.[8] ECOSOC would also allocate tasks as defined by the General Assembly among these institutions but also, to achieve a more efficient and reliable United Nations system, check and regularly control whether these organs correctly implement the Assembly's mandates. The objective is not to introduce suspicion among United Nations organs, but more efficiency and relevance through a more hierarchical – and somewhat more rigid – division of labour.

However, we would emphasize that this division of labour should be applied carefully. Indeed, if a separate office or organ were created for each task to be implemented, the phenomenon of institutional proliferation would not be checked. Thus, the division of labour has to be *rational*. By way of illustration, there is the example of the several committees of the Assembly, whose work overlaps[9] and, more importantly, also overlaps with the tasks assigned to ECOSOC (the case, as far as economic and social problems are concerned, of the Second and Third Committees). The Assembly allocates work to its various committees through its own General Committee, most of the committees usually being overburdened with numerous agenda items of marginal significance. Thus, in line with what has been said above, and following the logic of some recent changes – especially as a result of initiatives launched during the forty-fifth session of the General Assembly – two measures should be taken regarding the main committees:

A. In our view, only two committees should be retained – a political committee (which would include on its agenda peace-keeping, peace-making, etc., as well as legal matters), and a committee for financial and administrative matters; all economic, social, and related matters would be dealt with exclusively by ECOSOC. Of course, some good arguments not to alter the status quo could certainly be found; in particular, one strong argument

[8] See chapter seven.
[9] See chapter four.

in that direction is that all Member States are members of the several General Assembly committees, while ECOSOC – in many ways like the Security Council – is restricted to only a part of the United Nations membership. However, we believe that – in spite of this argument – there could be a compromise solution which eliminated the overlapping committees, while restructuring ECOSOC so as to include more members in its work – which, in a way, is today's *de facto* situation (if one also includes the States attending as observers);

B. The two remaining committees would have to be controlled and closely scrutinized by a vigilant General Committee, which would also continue to allocate the tasks of the Assembly to the two substantive committees. In addition, in order to give the General Committee more authority, it should meet continuously at the working level to carry out procedural chores, and to be able to follow up the work of the two committees; finally, like the Assembly itself, it should also meet regularly at the ministerial level in order to take policy decisions.

We are of course aware that the question of the reduction of the number of committees will not meet with an immediate consensus. But since drastic action is needed to solve the question of duplication and overlapping in the United Nations we still feel that the point should be made. An alternative would be to eliminate ECOSOC (a suggestion made by others). In our view it would be more practical to reduce the number of committees, despite the unlikelihood of the proposal being accepted in the near future.

The increased importance of the General Committee may also raise the question of its membership. We would not wish to see the present membership (the President, the Vice-presidents and the Chairmen of the main committees and ACABQ) changed drastically. But we feel that the decision on membership is one for the Member States themselves. Should the States insist on a change of membership, a solution could surely be found.

There is also need for some decentralization of responsibilities within the United Nations, in particular of those defined in economic and social areas by the Assembly. This decentralization should not be difficult to achieve because appropriate United Nations economic structures already exist. As early as 1947, a number of regional economic commissions were established. The first to come into existence was the Economic Commission for

Europe (ECE), based in Geneva, which has studied problems affecting the whole of the European economy, East as well as West, and published many technical studies in specialized fields. Following the break-up of the Soviet Union and the resurging importance of the Newly Independent States, Malta has been urging ECE to give more attention to the Mediterranean area. Not long after, the Economic Commission for Latin America (ECLA) was created, and based in Santiago in Chile to perform similar functions in that area. A little later the Economic Commission for Asia and the Far East, subsequently renamed the Economic and Social Commission for Asia and the Pacific (ESCAP) was established in Bangkok; the Economic Commission for Africa (ECA), in Addis Ababa; and finally, the Economic and Social Commission for Western Asia (ESCWA), with its headquarters in Baghdad, now operating from Amman. All of these bodies undertake continuing studies of the economic problems in their areas, organize conferences among Governments of the region in specialized fields and commission a large number of reports by experts from the regions.

Overall: 'The regional character of these commissions has given them a unity and coherence which their parent body (ECOSOC) has lacked; their problems have in the main been real, not propagandistic, their studies and recommendations rooted in the needs of their area.'[10] However, on the other hand: 'Most of (their) work represents *study* of the problems, rather than an attempt to do much about them.'[11] Thus, theory rather than practice seems to predominate.

Nevertheless, this problem could be very simply solved by ECOSOC itself: indeed, it is up to that organ to endow these regional structures with the powers necessary to implement the economic or social measures decided upon and thus to decentralize the whole United Nations economic and social structure. This is another step that we should like to see taken. This is hardly new. Almost 20 years ago the General Assembly had already decided through resolution 32/197 that the Regional Economic Commissions should be actively involved at the economic and social levels: 'The regional commissions should be enabled fully to play their role under the authority of the General Assembly and ECOSOC as the main general economic and social

[10] Nicholas, *op. cit.*, p. 140.
[11] Luard, *supra*, p. 64.

development centres within the United Nations system for their respective regions, having due regard to the responsibilities of the specialized agencies and other United Nations bodies in specific sectoral fields and the coordinating role of the United Nations Development Programme in respect of technical cooperation activities.'[12] Due to United Nations internal politics, this resolution was never really implemented. The centre did not release enough resources and authority to the regional commissions. The Member States did nothing about this. It is now time, we believe, to reaffirm our commitment to the decentralization of all economic, social and related matters including technical cooperation activities to the regions. This decentralization of United Nations activities to the regional commissions should set the stage for the undertaking of further tasks by the commissions, particularly those undertaken by UNDP (including UNFPA), and selected activities of the specialized agencies which could be better coordinated at the regional rather than the global level.

Increasing the coordination and collaboration between United Nations organs or agencies is essential. The efficient collaboration of organs and agencies – and an integrated approach to today's global problems – requires a reorganization of United Nations coordinating bodies.

Day-to-day coordination of the United Nations system is entrusted to the Administrative Committee on Coordination (ACC), which is made up of the Secretary-General of the United Nations as Chairman and his opposite numbers in the agencies. It could be seen as a kind of international cabinet, but with the particular characteristic that each minister is responsible to a different parliament (i.e. the agency that he or she represents). It was set up in 1946 in response to a recommendation by ECOSOC itself, reflecting an awareness of how difficult it was for a remote, intermittently functioning, overloaded Council to keep a close and continuous watch over so many independent and international entities. ACC would be a crucial organ within a renewed United Nations system. We believe that fewer attempts at coordination would be needed in a more streamlined system which, because of its transparency, would not require the Secretary-General and Heads of Agencies to meet regularly. Observers of

---

[12] Resolution 32/197, General Assembly, section IV of the annexe.

ACC thought the half-day or so of closed political briefing between the Secretary-General and his senior colleagues made the costs of the trip to a Headquarters city worth it. With the advances in communications technology one can hardly say that any more. Of course matters would sometimes require the Secretary-General to consult with Heads of Agencies and vice-versa – but modern communications like teleconferencing provide such a luxury without taking the most senior of civil servants from their more urgent work for more than a few minutes. It is also cheaper than bringing the Executive Heads and their aides to a designated city for a two- or three-day meeting.

Overall, there is also a vital need for some intergovernmental body to ensure coordination. In theory, at programme level, it could be the CPC; however, this body needs to be given more importance by Member States. In addition, ACABQ, a committee made up of experts responsible for financial and budgetary matters, has seen its effectiveness increasingly deteriorating due to its over-politicization – Governments not always proposing members on the basis of qualifications. Thus, a Committee that was supposed to be purely technical is now tainted by politics.

The infrastructure necessary for coordination is already there and only needs some refocusing. CPC and ACABQ can supply the necessary coordination at the intergovernmental level, in the context of the Administrative and Financial Committee. With a more streamlined United Nations this should prove easier. On the other hand, a reconstructed ACC could supply the United Nations system's coordination. Occasional CPC/ACABQ/ACC high-level meetings could bond this coordination.

At the policy level, coordination is the responsibility of the Main Committees and Organs. In fact, one of the tasks of ECOSOC is supposed to be coordination and institutional co-operation although we have shown, in chapter four, that it has never been really effective in that area. Therefore, as pointed out in chapter seven, its role as a coordinating organ for United Nations economic or social agencies needs to be improved. Similarly, the General Assembly's main committees and, above all, its General Committee, need to have their coordinating role in their respective areas developed and reinforced.

The same may be said of other United Nations entities intended to coordinate particular areas such as humanitarian assistance. For example, the Department of Humanitarian Affairs

(DHA) was initially set up to, *inter alia*, coordinate emergency assistance, in areas in which organs such as UNICEF, UNHCR and others are involved. Instead, DHA became absorbed in its own operations, and is perceived to cooperate insufficiently with the other humanitarian institutions. DHA, and similar United Nations organs, should remember their original objectives and not deviate from them. That it may be necessary for DHA to field a limited number of staff to perform a coordination role is understandable but this should not develop into an operational role in the already crowded field of humanitarian assistance. In this connection, DHA should refrain from duplicating what UNHCR, UNICEF and others do so efficiently. Now is the time to refocus the work of DHA before it becomes too unwieldy and before too many countries develop a national interest in uncontrolled DHA expansion. DHA therefore fulfils an important coordination role in our Second Generation United Nations. If DHA does not rise to the occasion, the alternative would be for UNHCR or some other agency to do the job.

We are living in an interdependent world, and it has been so at least since the end of the Second World War and the creation of the United Nations. However, today, one must recognize the consequences of this fact, in particular *vis-à-vis* the United Nations. Indeed, in order to be truly universal, as it is in terms of membership, the Organization will also have to encompass global human affairs in a more integrated and coherent manner which so far it has failed to do. This is certainly the main challenge that the Organization must face in the coming years; and this is also the necessary prerequisite for its survival and continuance in a fairer world, based on the principles of solidarity, peace, freedom and prosperity.

It may take us some time to accept a break with tradition. It may even appear strange to come to terms with the fact that things can be managed differently at the United Nations and that they may actually work as intended.

NINE

NATIONAL VERSUS GLOBAL PRIORITIES AND TARGETS

Summary

Sometimes global priorities and targets do not coincide with national ones. Indeed, this may be one of the major reasons why the United Nations is not as effective as many people would wish. However, since the end of the Second World War, the extent of integration of societies and cultures has fundamentally altered perceptions of sovereignty and national interest. Today, more than ever, it is difficult to separate national from international affairs since many local events have ramifications that extend far beyond national borders. Moreover, non-State actors, especially non-governmental organizations, play an increasingly important role in shaping policies internationally. Also, the drastically altered geopolitical environment, especially since the end of the cold war, has changed substantially the significance of groupings such as the Non-Aligned Movement and the East-West blocs. As a result, rather than nation-States, regions will play an increasingly important role and it is hoped that it will be easier to build common understandings to bridge the gap between national and global priorities and targets. The trend towards regionalization should also be exploited by the United Nations. It is for this reason that we attach such importance in our proposals for a Second Generation United Nations to giving more responsibility to established regional institutions like OSCE. Along with this trend, the United Nations is called upon to take on an increasing number of wide-ranging tasks. Yet, in order to act effectively internationally, the Organization must be funded properly and countries must accept that the work of the United Nations is in every nation's interest. The end of the cold war offers a unique historical opportunity to reap the benefits of a peace dividend by diverting resources away from military purposes towards United Nations work on peace and development. This has not yet happened. Any reform of the United Nations system which fails to address the chronic financial crisis that it has been experiencing over the years will not succeed. Acceptance of United Nations restructuring by Member States will be the test of whether the gap between national and global priorities and targets can be bridged.

(a) *National vs. Global Affairs*

The United Nations was created in a world in which nation-States dominated international affairs. As long as national priorities were not affected negatively, Members allowed the United Nations to exist and to grow. As long as their own goals and purposes were served, Members supported the United Nations. This may be the main reason why we are faced today with so much disillusionment over the Organization. Member States must accept much of the responsibility for allowing it to stray off course.

The Charter represented a visionary approach toward the conduct of international affairs by treating political, economic, security and social issues as interrelated and empowering the United Nations to transcend problems arising from relations among States by pursuing broad goals, such as 'the economic and social advancement of all peoples'. Fifty years later, the concept of sovereignty and of independent States is under siege. Globalization and interdependence have become the order of the day, making it difficult to shield any one country from the effects of important events that occur in another. For example, severe currency fluctuations, in particular the recent decline in the value of the United States dollar, have repercussions globally and affect the prices of many products and the performance of many economies. Also, the flood of refugees fleeing from internal disturbance, such as the ethnic violence in the former Yugoslavia or in Rwanda, have affected many societies around the world.

Moreover, non-governmental organizations (NGOs) and other non-State actors exert a growing influence over the determination of policies internationally. One estimate puts the current number of NGOs at around 29,000 and growing.[1] These organizations represent no single country but people across national, cultural and political boundaries. This growing internationalization of civil society demands that States no longer conceive of themselves as closed entities, but open societies able to adapt to the strong winds of change.

These globalization and internationalization trends have been accompanied by a move towards regionalization, as people look increasingly to wider geographical entities than the nation-State for security and other purposes. This can be seen, for example, in the growth of inter-regional economic (and, increasingly, political) groupings such as the European Union (EU), the North American Free Trade Agreement (NAFTA) and the Asia-Pacific Economic Cooperation forum (APEC). Other regional groupings, such as OSCE, are working to ensure better regional security arrangements and cooperation. This is, in our view, is the world of the future which the United Nations of the future should heed and with which it should develop in harmony.

Increasingly, then, the United Nations will be called upon to address a variety of new and daunting challenges that cross national boundaries and bind different peoples together. Members of the United Nations, however, must mobilize the political will necessary to ensure success, and, in order to meet the challenges and ensure the success, must make sure that the financial integrity of the Organization is guaranteed.

(b) *Financial Support (Contributions to the United Nations System)*

That many events have domestic and international spillovers is one of the reasons that the United Nations has been increasingly called upon. But this unprecedented growth in the demand for United Nations services has strained seriously the financial resources of the Organization, especially with regard to the funding of peace-keeping operations. If, as we argued above, no country is sheltered fully from the effects of calamitous events in other countries, then all countries should realize that it is in their own interest, as well as the world's, to finance properly a reformed United Nations that can deal effectively and efficiently

---

[1] The Commission on Global Governance, *Our Global Neighbourhood*, Oxford University Press, Oxford, 1995, pp. 32–35.

with global problems. Better financing, coupled with improved efforts at efficient financial management within the United Nations, should ensure a relatively stable financial environment for the Organization.

The United Nations has suffered from a chronic financial crisis for much of its existence. This seriously undermines the efficacy of its work, discourages its staff and leads to an intolerable situation in which those that supply the most money exercise the most power. Some of the studies and reports on the United Nations have been devoted to this financial crisis. Of these, the Ford Foundation report (proposed by a group co-chaired by Shijuro Ogata and Paul Volcker) has been well-received and is considered to be the best plan to address the predicament.

The Ogata-Volcker proposals make several main points. First, they advocate dividing the United Nations expenditure into three categories: a regular budget financed by assessed contributions; peace-keeping financed by a separate assessment; and humanitarian and development activities financed mostly by voluntary contributions. Secondly, they would require Member States to pay dues in four quarterly instalments, instead of a single lump sum at the beginning of the year; and give the Organization the authority to charge interest on late payments. Thirdly, some countries should be encouraged to make their contribution earlier in the year. Fourthly, Member States should accept significantly increased peace-keeping costs over the next few years, and finance future costs from national defence budgets. Fifthly, the United Nations should create a $400 million revolving reserve fund for peace-keeping and consider the creation of a unified peace-keeping budget, financed by a single assessment.

However, it is clear from the United Nations' first fifty years that depending too much on the contributions of a single member (or a small number of members) is unacceptable for a global organization. As a result, alternative methods of financing must be explored, while maintaining the principle that no member should have a special voice or weight in the formulation of programmes and policies. In the meantime, Members that are in default should be penalized. For example, they should not be eligible for recruitment of their nationals and barred from receiving United Nations contracts. Ultimately, countries persistently in arrears should have their voting privileges suspended, as well as their eligibility to present candidates for posts or to bid for UN contracts and procurement.

One promising funding alternative is to adjust the relative levels of Members' contributions by increasing the amount contributed by middle-income countries and reviewing regularly their relative financial capabilities. This would narrow the gap between the largest contributors and others, effectively reducing the influence that these larger countries can exercise over the activities of the United Nations. Another set of ideas has been proposed by the Commission on Global Governance which includes James Tobin's suggestions for a tax on international currency transactions and proposals to introduce charges for common global resources such as sea and flight lanes and ocean fishing rights.

Another idea is to tap the large multinationals by charging them a reasonable fee for the maintenance by the United Nations and its programmes of a peaceful environment in which to operate. This should make perfect sense to firms, since the opportunity costs associated with, for example, having to cease operations in troubled areas and restart operations elsewhere are enormous and regularly made avoidable by United Nations activities.

A further idea is for the United Nations to receive a percentage of its large procurement and sub-contracting disbursements which now go to the major developed countries – sometimes exceeding the contributions that some of the major donors make to the United Nations.

Finally, another suggestion is to run the local United Nations offices on a commercial basis and to charge for services rendered, for example, in the organization of donor conferences. This will be always on the understanding that free assistance to the least developed countries and other developing countries continues to be paramount in the work of the Organization.

These ideas may appear radical today (as income tax appeared radical earlier this century) but whatever the specific financing reforms, it is important that the financial integrity of the United Nations be secured by raising revenue and reducing costs wherever possible.

With the end of the cold war, we believe that the world is presented with a unique historical opportunity. For decades, countries on both sides of the East-West divide spent untold trillions of dollars to secure themselves against any possible aggression. This atmosphere of fear was dissolved with the fall of the Berlin Wall and it is now time for the world to reap the benefits of a peace dividend. Reductions in military expenditure, especially among the largest countries, should be encouraged and part of the savings should be dedicated to ensuring that global peace and development are properly pursued within a reformed United Nations. Yet, the peace dividend remains elusive and, once again, political will is needed to transcend entrenched habits and encourage countries to divert resources away from war-making capabilities to capabilities for making peace.

Along with these proposals for improving the financial resources available to the United Nations, prudent financial management practices should be independently developed and closely followed by the United Nations system. United Nations organs and agencies should be encouraged, especially in the current climate of austerity, to improve the quality of their work. General guidelines, including those outlined by a Swedish government working paper,[2] can provide clear, yet flexible, direction for the management of scarce United Nations resources. Such guidelines may include individual assessment of each organization, according to revised budget proposals, so that the planning and budget process, and the analyses of results, are sufficiently transparent from the point of view of Member States and of sufficiently high quality to ensure, within reasonable limits, that resources are used efficiently. By following prudent financial management practices, the United Nations can instil in Member States the confidence necessary to ensure that contributions are made willingly and in good faith.

In the current global environment, devoid of the paralysing East-West cold war and characterized increasingly by the phenomena of globalization and regionalization, a restructured and properly funded United Nations that can effectively bring together societies and peoples to help bridge the gap between national and global priorities and targets is essential. Whether countries accept the restructuring of the United Nations will be the test of whether the gap between national and global priorities and targets can be bridged.

[2] Ministry of Foreign Affairs, Sweden, *Financial Management in International Organizations*, Stockholm, 1994.

TEN

A GUARANTEE FOR PEACE
IN FREEDOM

Summary

We must now seize this historic opportunity and create a Second
Generation United Nations. This can be done by returning to the
basic principles of the Charter and the vision of the founders of
the Organization.

Our proposals for a Second Generation United Nations represent an attempt to learn from the past mistakes and shortcomings
of the Organization and, indeed, the League of Nations before
it. One core lesson is that, in order to secure success in humanity's
search for peace and prosperity for all, countries need to overcome the tendency to favour national priorities and targets at
the expense of international goals which recognize the solidarity
of all peoples. Our proposals centre around a pre-eminent
General Assembly, a rejuvenated ECOSOC and a refocused
Trusteeship Council. We believe that these, along with the
detailed changes in the structure and functioning of the United
Nations system to make it more efficient and just, should lead
to the revitalization of the Organization fifty years after its
inception.

We suggest that detailed and specific recommendations be
proposed for adoption by the fifty-first session of the General
Assembly, which should be designated the 'enabling' or
'implementing' session. The session should also designate 1997
as the Year of the Second Generation United Nations. The time
for studies and reflection should be over. It is now time for
action.

(a) *Conclusions*

We have argued throughout that we must seize this historic opportunity to revitalize the United Nations system and create a Second Generation United Nations. We believe that this can be done by returning to the basic principles of the Charter and the vision of the founders of the Organization. This includes first and foremost a pre-eminent, though not exclusive, role for the General Assembly, especially in the area of peace and security, which can be supported by high-level summits and by the institution of an Assembly in continuous session. Also, a better division of labour between the Assembly, the Secretariat and the Security Council can guarantee an optimal and efficient use of resources. But efficiency alone, without relevance, is not sufficient.

It is clear that the United Nations has not functioned to the expectations of its Member States. It has not evolved to reflect the needs and changes of a world different from the days of its inauguration in San Francisco. We feel that the United Nations can change and adapt without having fundamentally to alter the Charter. What is lacking at the moment is, in order of importance, political will, relevance and efficiency. Members allowed the United Nations to grow unchecked – as long as their national priorities were not affected adversely. Members supported the United Nations as long as it served their own goals and purposes. This, however, does not constitute real political will. Where there was concerted political will – as in the case of Namibia, decolonization and the struggle against apartheid – there was success. However, there are too many examples of failure where the lack of political will doomed all good intentions by the United Nations. The political will, of course, has to come from the Member States.

Once the political will is present, the United Nations has to be relevant and responsive to the wishes of the majority and implement decisions taken. This underlines the importance of making the General Assembly, with its principle of universal membership, the pre-eminent organ. At present, the General Assembly, the Security Council, one of its major organs, and the Bretton Woods institutions, part of the United Nations system, diverge frequently on policy and other matters.

Many Governments have blamed the United Nations for being

too unwieldy and unable to coordinate its many activities. We agree that there is room to improve efficiency. This means taking difficult decisions regarding the elimination of some organs, agencies and programmes, while down-sizing or altering others and abolishing duplication. Too many entities have emerged in various fields, including that of economic development, and there needs to be a re-evaluation of their roles and mandates to reduce or eliminate those which are truly unnecessary and strengthen those that remain. The exercise should include the decentralization of United Nations economic, social and related activities to give regional commissions a greater role. More autonomy in operational activities should be accorded to the Bretton Woods institutions and the United Nations Secretariat divested of all responsibilities in this regard. Moreover, in this reformed United Nations, there must be a solid commitment to a close and substantive collaboration among agencies and organs. Importantly, this includes the notions of specialization, complementarity and a rational division of labour, or assigning specific tasks and missions to those agencies or organs that are best qualified in their particular field. The Bretton Woods institutions must receive policy guidelines from the General Assembly.

Member States, however, must also accept responsibility for improving coordination of their own policies. The conflict between national and international priorities and targets must be overcome by Member States. Through the phenomena of globalization and interdependence, all countries are linked and none are spared the effects of major problems or disturbances. Moreover, Member States must guarantee the financial viability of a reformed United Nations in order to ensure the necessary preconditions for its success. This guarantee of adequate resources is crucial.

The importance of the staff and the quality of the leadership of the United Nations cannot be over-emphasized. Again there are proposals in the cited studies, as well as in our own, that should be considered seriously. Ultimately there is no place in the United Nations system for a heterogeneity of staff conditions and policies.

A central concept that is consistent throughout our study is that the United Nations should adopt a more comprehensive and integrated approach to world problems and issues and that there can be no true peace in the world without development. In other words, peace is not just the absence of war but a more holistic process that includes social, economic and political development. Our recommendations are being made with this in mind.

(b) *Recommendations*

The following, in summary, are our proposals for a Second Generation United Nations:

I. A *General Assembly* that meets in regular session throughout the year targeting political, economic, social, human rights and other issues at the working, ministerial and summit levels;

II. A *General Committee* also in session all year round, mostly at the working level (permanent representatives) but, when needed, at the ministerial level. This Committee would be strengthened by having the ability (in consultation with the Security Council) to field prompt fact-finding missions and a degree of intervention capability sufficient to prevent crises from either occurring or deteriorating;

III. Two other *main Committees*, one for Political, Peace-keeping and related matters and the other for Administration and Finance (all other Committees will be phased out gradually);

IV. A *Security Council* with some changes regarding its functioning and membership (provided that it does not increase the veto power), sharing with the General Committee responsibility for a multinational force that can monitor situations and provide a rapid-reaction measure in case of crises until a larger force (if necessary) can be mobilized;

V. An *ECOSOC* for Economic, Social and related matters, but with Human Rights transferred to the new Trusteeship Council. In particular, a redefined relationship with the Bretton Woods institutions (themselves reformed, possibly to include the take-over of operational development matters from UNDP and the United Nations Secretariat) in order to increase substantially the regulatory authority of ECOSOC (on behalf of the United Nations General Assembly) over these institutions and to consolidate and increase the resources available for development assistance and technical co-operation;

VI. A *Trusteeship Council* to hold in trust the heritage of present and future generations, the environment, the resources of the sea and the seabed; the rights of future generations and human rights, including the safeguarding of the sovereign rights of peoples in situations of complete breakdown of the organs of the State;

VII. A *Secretariat* that implements and coordinates policy, with a Secretary-General selected on the basis of a set of strict criteria and assisted by three Deputy Secretaries-General: a Deputy Secretary-General for Political, Security and Peace Affairs, a Deputy Secretary-General for International Economic Cooperation and Sustainable Development and a Deputy Secretary-General for Administrative, Management and Conference Services. A Secretariat that delegates operational activities (including technical cooperation) to the Bretton Woods institutions, to the Regional Economic Commissions, and to the specialized agencies;

VIII. A decentralized United Nations that would rely to a much greater extent on regional institutions. For instance, as already proposed by Malta in Helsinki II, the CSCE (now OSCE) has become the regional arrangement for peace-keeping in terms of Chapter VIII of the Charter of the United Nations. This would also involve other regional organizations following the same OSCE model. In the area of economic, social and related matters, the United Nations would decentralize the work to the five Regional Economic Commissions.

The major elements of the recommendations are presented in diagram 3, Second Generation United Nations, below.

Finally, we believe that the time for study and reflection is now over and that detailed and specific recommendations should be prepared for adoption by the fifty-first session of the General Assembly which should be designated the 'enabling' or 'implementing' session. This session should also designate 1997 as the Year of the Second Generation United Nations.

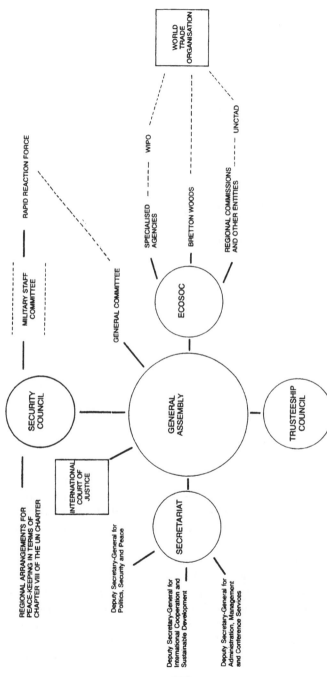

Diagram 3: Second Generation United Nations

EPILOGUE

BEYOND THE SECOND GENERATION UNITED NATIONS

Summary

The debate on the reform of the United Nations should not be allowed to run out of steam. It is understandable that sometimes the frustrations of the inability of the United Nations to make concrete progress in this regard can be discouraging. There should be, however, no letting up in our bold efforts to ensure that the United Nations truly consolidates its promise in the interest of the people it represents.

The United Nations was born of the political commitment of some States. It was however intended as a universal institution - universal in terms of its membership, and also universal in terms of the principles and values it projected and protected.

The Charter of the United Nations, itself, instils a sense of belonging in the peoples of the world. We cannot shy away from the responsibility we have towards, *"we the peoples"*. We know of the gap between rhetoric and action in this regard. We have referred in the text to the struggle between national and global priorities. We have emphasised the importance of relevance over efficiency. We think that eventually we would succeed to have a better United Nations for the future because there is no other easier alternative.

We therefore wish to continue in our efforts to make the United Nations an Organisation better equipped to meet the aspirations of the peoples it represents. In particular the purpose of the book is to demonstrate how relevance needs to be built into both the workings of the Institution through changes in the methods employed by the United Nations, and also through a re-thinking in terms of the manner in which the principles of the Organisation are reflected through its mandate.

The Book on the *Second Generation United Nations* was first published in 1997 when the debate on United Nations reform was at its peak. In January 1997 a new Secretary General of the United Nations was appointed and found a rich harvest of reform proposals which resulted from an initiative during the forty-fifth General Assembly under a Maltese Presidency.

The proposals of the *Second Generation United Nations* formed part of this rich harvest, and in fact, some were reflected in the Secretary-General's own Report[1], *Renewing The United Nations: A Programme of Reform* which was issued on 14 July 1997. The Secretary General had at his disposal a wealth of analysis and recommendations, the most important of which came as a result of a number of *ad hoc* committees which were established soon after the 45th Session of the General Assembly and which dealt with a number of important sectors and subjects of the United Nations. Work on some of these sectors and subjects, like on the Security Council, is still continuing in some form or another.

An overview of the developments since the book was published

A number of developments have taken place in the field of reform since the book was first published. The 45th Session of the General Assembly remains a landmark, in that the very principle of reform was revived during that time. Uniquely

---

[1] A\51\950, 14\07\1997

poised with the challenge created with the end of the Cold War, the United Nations could start to take a serious look at being more pro-active. Since then, the efforts launched during the 45th Session of the General Assembly resulted in tangible expressions taking the form of a deliberating process discussing different aspects of reform.

Some of the *Ad Hoc* Committees on United Nations reform under the President of the General Assembly continued their work and some submitted their conclusions to the General Assembly. Other developments in the area of United Nations reform like the comprehensive Report of the Secretary-General mentioned above may be considered as landmarks, although the implementation of the recommendations leave a lot to be desired.

The open-ended High Level Group on the Strengthening of the United Nations System, was the last of the five closed-door groups created to address different aspects of United Nations reform. This Group created in September 1995 dealt with the General Assembly and the Secretariat. It presented its comprehensive recommendations to the General Assembly on 1 May 1997. Other groups dealt with, the Agenda for Peace; the Agenda for Development, Finance and of course the Security Council. The group on the Security Council submitted its recommendations[2] to the General Assembly in September 1998 again with no breakthrough. The salient points of all these groups are worth keeping in mind; although without exception very little of a concrete nature had been implemented.

Some of the Groups were split further into sub-groups. The working group on the Agenda for Peace, for example, had four sub-groups, with only two sub-groups ending up making some kind of recommendations. The sub-group on Co-ordination made recommendations on troop-contributing States, regional arrangements, NGOs and co-ordination within the United Nations System itself. The only other sub-group with any significant results was the sub-group on United Nations Imposed Sanctions. In response to the Secretary-General's report entitled *Supplement to an Agenda for Peace*

---

[2] A/AC.247/1998/WP.1/Rev.2, 11/08/98

(03\01\1995), the sub-group made some recommendations[3] on the subject of Sanctions, emphasising the conditions that ought to be respected and the humanitarian aspects of the sanctions.

The Working Group on the Financial Situation of the United Nations discussed three inter-related issues[4], without being able to propose concrete recommendations to the General Assembly. These issues were the cash-flow situation, the payments of contributions in full and on time and the scale of assessment.

The Working Group on an Agenda for Development did substantial work in the form of an *Agenda for Development*, which was adopted by the General Assembly[5] . This interesting document dwells heavily on the co-ordination within the United Nations System and gives a role to the *civil society*. This document, however, typical of United Nations consensus documents of this kind skirts the issue of changes in the relationship between the United Nations and the Bretton Woods Institutions.

Another Working Group which produced substantial material in areas where there seemed to be consensus was the Group on the Strengthening of the United Nations System[6]. Some of the recommendations of this Group deal with ways of "Improving the capacity of the General Assembly to discharge effectively its functions, role and powers and of the Secretariat to carry out effectively and efficiently the mandates of inter-governmental processes with the necessary transparency and accountability."

These recommendations, if implemented would certainly help towards a better and more efficient functioning of the United Nations but fail, in our opinion to address the question of relevance. Admittedly this is not an easy issue, especially when one needs the agreement of all the Member States to adopt recommendations by consensus.

---

[3] WGAP\96\2, 06\09\1996
[4] WGFS\28, 15\12\1995 and WGFS\30, 26\01\1996
[5] A\AC.250\1, 16\06\1997
[6] WGUNS\CRP.16, 02\06\1997

President after President of the General Assembly regretted the fact that hardly anything substantial came out of these *ad hoc* working groups to enable the General Assembly to take some significant decisions on United Nations reform. In addition, the set of recommendations in the Secretary-General's Report, referred to above, which required Governments' approval were not acted upon.

This stalemate came as no surprise since as early as 6 May 1998 the General Assembly had already deferred action on most of the reform proposals of the Secretary-General and there was never any expectation that the *ad hoc* working groups would come up with proposals of any significance that the Assembly could act upon.

Only one proposal of the Secretary-General, to designate the 55th General Assembly in the year 2000, as the Millennium General Assembly details on which were to be discussed later, was accepted in principle. In this context it may be recalled that it was recommended in the *Second Generation United Nations* that a future General Assembly should be designated as the 'enabling or implementing' Assembly and that the year of that Assembly would also be designated the year of the Second Generation United Nations.

All the Assembly did in May 1998 was to defer several proposals mainly of an administrative and financial nature to its Fifth Committee. These proposals included proposals on the Revolving Credit Fund, the Core Resources for Development, the Development Account, Sunset Provisions and Pilot Projects. Some of these proposals like the streamlining of the Agenda of the General Assembly were also dealt with in the *Second Generation United Nations.* Among these proposals was also the proposal on the need to make better use of the Trusteeship Council on the lines of the Malta recommendations on this body as also reflected in the *Second Generation United Nations*.

The Secretary-General, himself was much quicker than the General Assembly and by same period of May 1998 had already made substantial changes in the Secretariat, mainly of an administrative and efficiency nature.

EPILOGUE

The highlights of the Secretary General's proposals

The Secretary-General issued his report, entitled *RENEWING THE UNITED NATIONS: A PROGRAMME FOR REFORM* on 14 July 1997. He made three kinds of recommendations. First dealing with administrative and financial management of the Secretariat, programmes and funds, which he started implementing immediately. The second dealt with recommendations which needed Government agreement and the third with longer term proposals like the one on the Trusteeship Council which resembles very closely Malta's blueprint for that Council.

The Secretary-General's report was received with much enthusiasm but as indicated above the results so far have not been encouraging. His original plea for relevancy fell much short of expectations and the results, as in other past efforts for reform have been in the area of efficiency only. This, as in the past would raise the concern that what the United Nations needs is to be relevant before being efficient. Or, as indicated on various occasions in the past by the President of the 45th Session of the General Assembly 'efficiency without relevance is a step backwards'.[7]

Some final comments and looking towards the future

It appears that the Secretary-General's proposals do not seem to be making much headway and any progress has been only in the area of administrative reform. Other recommendations like those of some of the *ad hoc* working groups and those from outside the United Nations have not fared any better. This is clearly not enough. We do not expect that any one book or any one person would have all the answers and solutions for a better United Nations. We also do

---

[7] For more details on the highlights of the Secretary-General's proposals and a comparison of his proposals to those of the *Second Generation United Nations* refer to *A Better United Nations for the New Millennium*, by Kamil Idris and MichaelBartolo, published by Kluwer Law International, pp 24-27

not expect, that the United Nations can solve all mankinds' problems. But it is in everyone's interest to have the best possible United Nations. Furthermore, reform in the United Nations cannot be seen in isolation of what is happening in the World around us. Apart from the political scenarios mentioned in the Preface, one cannot ignore the economic and social developments enveloping us. Globalisation and liberalisation of the world economy seem to be now on an accelerating and unstoppable trajectory. The United Nations of the new Millennium must assist the developing countries, and particularly the least developed among them, to share in the gains from these phenomena. It is not so now. We think that the ideas and proposals of the *Second Generation United Nations* still present the best core elements for a better United Nations for the future. Some of these ideas have already been developed further elsewhere[8]. May be it is time now for the Millennium Assembly to show the political will of the Member States by calling for the General Conference referred to in the Preface.

---

[8] See *op.cit.*

ANNEXE I
Summary of previous proposals

Since the creation of the United Nations, the proposals for reforming the Organization have come to form a rich body of literature. The following is a summary of a number of these studies, some of which were mentioned in chapter three.

Bertrand, Maurice, 'Some Reflections on Reform of the United Nations', Joint Inspection Unit, United Nations, Geneva, 1985, JIU/REP/85/9.

In this report, the aim of the reforms is to build up an 'economic United Nations' parallel to the existing 'political United Nations'. For this to be achieved, Maurice Bertrand proposed the following:[1]

– Restructure entirely the United Nations development organs so as to integrate them at the regional or sub-regional levels. The creation of 'Regional Development Agencies' would allow the concentration of development resources on specific problems.

– Create a centralized interdisciplinary Secretariat, coupled with small sectoral secretariats within each Agency.

– Establish an Economic Security Council (ESC), dealing solely with economic issues. This Council would replace the duplicated fora of ECOSOC and UNCTAD and would represent the major Powers and regions of the world system.

– Discontinue the Administrative Committee on Coordination (ACC) and replace it with a 'Council-Commission' structure. This arrangement would foster cooperation between secretariats and

---

[1] It should be noted that some of Maurice Bertrand's proposals were revised in the years that followed his initial report.

inter-governmental organs, the former being represented by commission members and the latter by national Ministers or members of the Economic Security Council.

– Increase the delegations' representatives to two higher level officials: a political ambassador and an economic representative from the Ministry of Finance and Economic affairs of each Member State.

The reform process represented in this report was to be achieved in three steps: 1) detail a blueprint for a reformed United Nations; 2) immediately implement preliminary reforms; 3) draft a transition plan. The blueprint would feature the legal aspects of the new organs created, while the transition plan would define how to transfer resources to the regional development agencies. The transition plan would also detail how the various United Nations secretariats and agencies would be reorganized to concentrate economic services under one division rather than being fragmented into Specialized Agencies.

Renninger, John P., 'Improving the UN System', in *Journal of Development Planning* **No. 17, 1987, pp. 85–111.**

In this study, John Renninger put forth the following suggestions:

ECOSOC:
– Assign ECOSOC a limited number of functions for which it is solely responsible.[2] This measure would improve ECOSOC's performance with respect to coordinating and supervising international economic matters.

– Devote an entire ECOSOC regular session to only one or two issues and let the Second and Third Committee of the General Assembly handle the remaining questions. This would foster a genuine intellectual discussion.

International Civil Service:
– Revitalize the international civil service, a process which would be undertaken by Executive Heads through the Administrative Committee on Coordination (ACC).

– Implement a system for reviewing objectively the competence of the United Nations staff every five years.

---

[2] Renninger claimed that 'discussion' could be the main function of ECOSOC.

– Design a Staff Training Programme and possibly a UN Staff College.

– Ensure more rigorous recruitment practices in order to improve staff quality.

Nerfin, Marc, 'The Future of the UN System: Some Questions on the Occasion of an Anniversary', in *Development Dialogue,* **No. 1, 1985, pp. 5–29.**

Marc Nerfin's main suggestion was the establishment of a Three-Chamber United Nations in which decision-making power would be shared between the *Prince* (governments), the *Merchant* (economic powers) and the *Citizen* (civil society). A reformed United Nations system would preserve States' authority through the Prince Chamber, while the Merchant Chamber would incorporate multinational corporations as well as other economic players. Finally, the Citizen Chamber would represent international social actors, be they the people or their associations.

The UN in Development. Reform Issues in the Economic and Social Fields. A Nordic Perspective, Nordic UN Project 1991.

The proposals delineated in the Nordic UN Project aimed at reforming the fragmented operational activities for development. The Project focused mainly on the issues of governance and financing of development activities. Their concrete suggestions were as follows:

Governance:

– Revise the management structure as well as the system in place for financing development operations.

– Establish an International Development Council (IDC) in order to guide and coordinate the United Nations development activities.

– Create smaller governing bodies, based on universality and representative of development agencies through enhanced executive power.

Financing:

– Expand the funding formula of development activities to

assessed contributions from all Member States, negotiated pledges and the present voluntary contributions.

Boutros-Ghali, Boutros, *An Agenda for Peace*, United Nations, New York, A/47/277, 1992.

The *Agenda for Peace* focused mainly on international security issues and the means to improve preventive diplomacy, peace-keeping, peace-making and peace-building through the United Nations Organization.

Preventive Diplomacy:
– Multiply the use of fact-finding missions to increase the United Nations capacity for preventive actions.
– Strengthen the early warning system so as to assess effectively threats to peace.
– Encourage preventive deployment through humanitarian and security assistance which are all factors helping negotiation environments and thus conciliation.

Peace-making:
– Recognize the General Assembly's capacity to urge intervention when there is a threat to international peace.
– Reinforce the role of the International Court of Justice for the peaceful settlement of disputes.
– Identify a mechanism to mobilize necessary resources for peace-making.
– Establish permanent armed forces through contributions of the Member States.
– Develop a Military Staff Committee[3] as a peace-making and not a peace-keeping organ.
– Create Peace-Enforcement Units. The Units would consist of ready-made contingents available according to the needs of the Security Council.

Peace-keeping:
– Clarify the Member States' contribution of military personnel.
– Ameliorate the training of peace-keeping personnel.

---

[3] Under Chapter VII on the use of military force.

– Improve the capacities of the Secretariat's military staff.

– Establish a stock of peace-keeping equipment such as vehicles, communication devices and generators so that they are available from the onset of an operation.

Other Security-related Reforms:

– Promote peace-building through educational, cultural or economic exchanges and other technical assistance dealing with post-war reconstruction.

– Foster cooperation between United Nations and regional bodies when handling international conflicts.

– Set in motion meetings, involving head of States that are members of the Security Council, every alternate year so as to exchange views and foster cooperation.

Financing:

– Establish a revolving peace-keeping reserve fund.

– Ensure that, once the Security Council supports a new peace-keeping operation, the General Assembly immediately appropriates one-third of the estimated costs of the operation.

– Acknowledge that the Secretary-General may be compelled to place contracts without prior competition under special security circumstances.

Human Development Report 1992, Oxford University Press, Oxford, Chapter 5.

The UNDP's *Human Development Report 1992* put forward a series of proposals for reforming the United Nations. Some of them follow.

Financial and Economic Reforms:

– Create a Central World Bank in charge of a common currency, the maintenance of price and exchange rate stability and financing of assistance to developing countries. This could be achieved from a transformation of IMF into a manager of the international economy, while the World Bank would act as an intermediary between capital markets and developing countries.

– Merge GATT and UNCTAD into an International Trade Organization.

– Approve a world income tax to be redistributed from the developed to the developing countries.

– Adopt a new tax on the environment and replace military assistance by development assistance.

Multinational Corporations:

– Domestically, establish a conciliatory council in each multi-national corporation which would be composed of public and private sector delegates.

– Internationally, agree upon standards of behaviour for multinational corporations so as to allow United Nations regulations to be enforced.

Evans, Gareth, *Cooperating for Peace*, Allen & Unwin Pty. Ltd., St-Leonards (Australia), 1993.

Gareth Evans, then Australian Foreign Minister, put forward some of the following recommendations for reforming the United Nations:

Preventive Diplomacy:

– Create Peace and Security Resource Centres to carry out preventive diplomacy and dispute resolution.

– Improve the quality, speed and reliability of information-gathering as well as political analyses to identify potential threats to peace.

– Train the Secretariat in dispute resolution.

– Create preventive diplomacy teams responsible for high-level negotiations and which would be based in New York and in Peace and Security Resource Centres.

– Incorporate preventive deployment in the United Nations strategies for ensuring peace, preferably through regional organizations.

Peace-keeping:

– Finance peace-keeping operations mandated by the United Nations directly from the Organization's budget, while other operations' costs should be borne by their initiators.

– Commit the Peace-Keeping Reserve Fund to its initial role: bear the start-up costs of new operations. The Fund should also receive increased funding.

– Set up a unified budget for peace-keeping interventions thereby allowing a rapid deployment of forces.

– Mandate an independent commission to improve the Secretariat's organization and planning.

– Increase peace-keeping effectiveness by relying initially on the peace-keeping forces of countries already cooperating militarily, thereby allowing an early deployment.

– Create equipment stocks to reduce intervention delays.

– Expand the capacity of small planning groups within the Department of Peace Operations in order to meet the increasing demand for peace-keeping operations.

– Establish a General Staff in charge of planning and managing peace-keeping operations.

Secretariat:

– Appoint four Deputy Secretaries-General in order to free the Secretary-General and allow him to focus on priority tasks. Each Deputy Secretary-General would be responsible for a different area: peace and security, economic and social, humanitarian and administration and management.[4] The sections acting under each Deputy Secretary-General would amalgamate the numerous existing organs responsible for either security, economic and social, humanitarian or administrative functions.

Security Council:

– Expand membership of the Security Council without linking this to a veto multiplication.

Financing:

– Solve the funding problem by strengthening Article 19 of the Charter stating that voting rights can cease if a Member Country is in arrears.

– Adopt a tax on international air travel.

Agenda for Development, **United Nations, A/48/935, 6 May 1994.**

The *Agenda for Development* emphasized the link between world peace and international development, thus the relevance of social

---

[4] It is to be noted that these suggestions were adapted from Childers and Urquhart, 'Towards a More Effective United Nations', in *Development Dialogue*, No. 1–2, 1991.

development for an organization such as the United Nations. People, it suggested, must participate actively in formulating their own goals and their voice must be heard in decision-making bodies. In addition to guidelines for thought and action by each State, specific recommendations for reform included:

– Grant special attention to find mechanisms to increase policy coherence and coordination among the development organs of the United Nations. Enhanced coordination could be achieved by designing development projects and the use of financial resources based on the 'country strategy' (UNDP). Also, the Resident Coordinator system should be strengthened.

– In particular, better coordination and cooperation should be pursued between the United Nations and the Bretton Woods institutions.

– Revitalize ECOSOC to prevent the overlaps and duplication of United Nations development bodies.

– To achieve sustainable economic development, governments should make development issues as much a priority as security concerns.

Childers, E. and Urquhart, B., *Renewing the UN System,* **Dag Hammarskjöld Foundation, Uppsala, 1994.**

To a great extent, *Renewing the UN System* built on the previous recommendations made by Childers and Urquhart. The following are old and new ideas submitted by the authors.

Secretariat:
– Appoint four Deputy Secretaries-General responsible for international Economic Cooperation and Sustainable Development, Humanitarian Affairs, Political Security and Peace Affairs, and Administration and Management. This new structure would absorb the bodies under the current fragmented United Nations system.

– Create a Documentation unit providing economic and social reports.

General Assembly and Other Organs:
– Schedule annual theme meetings for ECOSOC and allow for a question period in the General Assembly.

– Concentrate all development assistance into one United Nations System Office based in any developing country. This office would include members of UNDP, UNICEF, UNFPA, bearing in mind the ultimate goal to develop a single country programme.

– Decentralize the governance of UN operational activities at the regional level.

– Establish a single UN Development Authority, headed by the Deputy Secretary-General.

Bretton Woods Institutions:

– Organize a Monetary, Trade and Finance Conference to revise the IMF based on a more equitable arrangement, establish a genuine global International Trade Organization and develop equitable soft-loan facilities. This would lead to the creation of three equitable specialized agencies.

New Organs:

– Transform the Trusteeship Council into the Council on Diversity, Representation and Governance.[5] The Council would be a forum for minority groups to express their views, as well as a vehicle to correct existing boundaries, and suggests ways for moving societies from a traditional centralist State. The Council would also manage petitions, which could then be referred to any human rights body.

– Create a United Nations Parliámentary Assembly in which people's representatives would be democratically elected. The representatives would express citizen's views on the United Nations role on the international scene, use their influence to shape international policies, and maintain vigilance on the management and financing of the Organization.

– Establish a UN System Consultative Board responsible for ensuring the cohesion and effectiveness of the United Nations. The Board, assisted by the Administrative Committee on Coordination, would comprise bureaux of ECOSOC and agencies.

– Organize a UN Humanitarian Security Police ensuring safe transport and supply as well as general protection of UN and NGO emergency staff. This body would be constituted from a pool of volunteer national police forces.

---

[5] This is only an indicative title.

– Create a commission to improve the United Nations Civil Service and establish a UN Staff College to train international civil servants.

– Transform the mandate of the Administrative Committee on Coordination and rename it as Executive Committee of the United Nations system. It would ensure the coherence of United Nations actions and decisions.

– Appoint an independent 'ombuds-panel' on the Human rights performance of the United Nations in order to monitor respect of human rights within the Organization.

Human Development Report 1994, **Oxford University Press, Oxford.**

The proposals of the *Human Development Report 1994* complement the recommendations put forward in the *Human Development Report* published two years before. The fresh reform proposals are the following:

Creation of a World Government:
– Transform specialized United Nations organs into world ministries in such a way that, for example, FAO would become the world Ministry for Agriculture.

– Empower the world Ministry of Finance with a revenue-raising authority through a mandatory world levy in order to provide resources for the other world Ministries.

– Establish a world police authorized to bring States before the International Court of Justice.

– Create two world authorities, one responsible for oceans and the other in charge of space issues.

United Nations Organs:
– Restructure ECOSOC to give it more control and management power over development resources.

– Create an Economic Security Council, dealing with issues such as poverty and unemployment, thereby enlarging the notion of security into an economic one.

– With respect to collective security, revise and enlarge Chapter VII of the United Nations Charter so as to allow the Organization to intervene in intra-State conflicts.

– Reform technical assistance methods by providing the financial resources directly to the country concerned and yield its decision power on the use of these funds.

***State of the United Nations: Decline or Regeneration in the Next Fifty Years*, The Stanley Foundation, Santa Fe, June 1994.**

To regenerate the United Nations, it was suggested in this report that the United Nations system be given a new mandate as well as assimilate a mixture of fundamental reconfigurations, long-term reforms and near-term adjustments.

Future Mandates:
– Create universal norms and standards, developing by the same token international law, in areas such as poverty dislocation, women's rights and environmental degradation.
– Strengthen the United Nations involvement in collective security and peace operations as well as preventive diplomacy and cooperative security.[6]
– Define 'security' in terms of economic and social progress, in addition to political and military terms, thus the need to develop new models of security.
– Fight root causes of conflicts by focusing efforts on capacity-building: promote local development, human rights, conflict resolution and democratization.
– Increase the democratization for the 'historically disenfranchised', including the participation of NGOs in the United Nations forum.

Fundamental Reorganization:
– Create a global executive body composed of major powers and regional representatives of smaller countries. This body would be responsible for security, economic and social matters.
– Establish a representative parliament, composed either of national parliamentarians or directly-elected representatives.
– Develop accepted principles and corresponding review mechanisms in the spheres of human rights, democracy, minority protection and arms reduction.

[6] Cooperative security is defined as 'preventive in nature, focusing on internal unrest, population explosion, migration, environmental degradation, and poverty' (p. 21).

Long-term Reforms:

– Develop means to enforce arrears payments. Examine other methods of financing such as global taxation.

– Replace ECOSOC by an Economic Security Council with a similar size and operating procedure as the Security Council.

– Strengthen the United Nations judicial process by codifying the law and thereby strengthening the United Nations power of intervention in failed States.

– Improve the quality of the international civil service through a merit-based, dedicated and career-oriented system.

– Change public opinion of the United Nations' efficacy in more positive terms.

Near-term Adjustments:

– Improve coordination of United Nations organs and agencies, including the Bretton Woods institutions.

– Open the United Nations system by permitting greater NGO inputs as well as increasing the information flow.

– Increase United Nations military response, possibly through the creation of standby forces as established in Article 43 of the Charter and/or through a standing volunteer rapid deployment force.

– Enlarge the United Nations human rights machinery.

– Consolidate the United Nations leadership in arms control measures through the expansion of the UN Registry of Conventional Arms and the creation of a High Commissioner for Arms Control.

– Highlight cooperation with regional organizations by increasing communication with these organizations.

Our Global Neighbourhood, Commission on Global Governance, Geneva, 1995.

The Commission on Global Governance detailed in this book the reforms necessary to increase global security and governance through the United Nations. The specific recommendations are as follows:

Security:

– Amend the United Nations Charter to allow the international community to intervene when international security is endangered.

– Create a Council of Petitions entrenching the right of petition by non-State actors, allowing them to bring security matters to the attention of the Security Council.

– Improve peace-keeping through: 1) the creation of Consultative Committees for each peace-keeping operation; and 2) the active involvement of the permanent members of the Security Council in peace-keeping operations.

– Establish a United Nations Volunteer Force to deal with the first stage of a crisis and, by the same token, back up preventive diplomacy by reinforcing a United Nations threat of intervention.

General Assembly and Other Organs:

– Organize regular theme sessions and consolidate the budget authority of the General Assembly.

– Create an Annual Forum of Civil Society comprising Civil Society Organizations accredited to the General Assembly.

– Appoint a Senior Adviser on Women's Issues in the Office of the Secretary-General and in the Specialized Agencies.

– Empower the Trusteeship Council with responsibility for environmental questions.

– Concerning the International Court of Justice (ICJ), appoint judges for only one ten-year term and screen potential members on the basis of objectivity and jurisprudential skills. Give the Secretary-General of the United Nations the right to refer matters to the ICJ. Failing compliance by Member States with an ICJ ruling, the Security Council should enforce the decision under Article 94 of the Charter. Create an International Criminal Court.

Security Council:

– Firstly, transform the current membership so as to incorporate five new permanent members (two from industrial countries and three from Asia, Africa and Latin America). The number of non-permanent members would be raised to thirteen and the required votes for a decision to pass would be increased to fourteen. In this initial stage, there should also be an agreement on phasing out the veto.

– Secondly, review completely the membership composition of the Security Council taking into account changing circumstances and including arrangements on veto abolition.

Organs Discontinued:
– Discontinue ECOSOC, and review bodies such as UNCTAD and UNIDO, with a view to possibly discontinuing them as well.

Financial and Economic Reforms:
– Establish an Economic Security Council (ESC), involving high-level officials, that would pilot economic, social and environment-related activities. This new body would ensure the consistency between policy goals of international organizations, especially with respect to Bretton Woods institutions and the World Trade Organization.
– Adopt a GDP figure based on purchasing power parity as a basis for weighting national votes within the Bretton Woods institutions.
– Enlarge the IMF low-conditionality compensatory finance. In addition, the Fund should release new issues of Special Drawing Rights and increase its support of nominal exchange rates.
– Achieve consensus on a global taxation scheme on the use of global resources such as flight-lanes, sea lanes and ocean fishing areas. In addition, consider the possibility of a tax on international financial transactions and a tax on multinational companies.

Reforming the United Nations, **South Centre, Geneva, 1995.**

In *Reforming the United Nations*, the South Centre insisted that any reform return to the fundamental principles entrenched in the Charter: democracy, accountability and respect for diversity. To reinvigorate the United Nations, the Centre called for the following reforms:

Democracy:
– Establish a 'fully accountable' Security Council appointed by the General Assembly and based on democratic principles.
– Convey more democracy to the Bretton Woods institutions: revise their mandate and functions back to their original aims.
– Find new and stable sources of financing following the examination of alternative approaches and proposals. Meanwhile, adopt mechanisms to ensure arrears payment and promote democratic revenue-raising.

Economic Reforms:
  – Transfer the leadership in international economic issues to the United Nations by uniting all agencies concerned with international economic policy, including IBRD, IMF and WTO.
  – Make the Economic and Social Council fully responsible for economic security, possibly through the creation of a smaller ECOSOC body in charge of policy and operational matters.
  – Create a regulatory body for transnational corporations.
  – Establish an independent commission to revitalize the international civil service. In addition, grant the United Nations civil service a voice on issues taken up by the Organization.
  – Increase UNCTAD and UNIDO institutional and financial support.

The United Nations in its Second Half Century, Independent Working Group on the Future of the United Nations, Summer 1995.

The bulk of the proposals put forth by the Independent Working Group on the Future of the United Nations concerns the creation of three councils focusing respectively on security, economic affairs and social issues.

Security Council and Security Issues:
  – Expand membership from 15 to 23 members, with a maximum of five new permanent members.
  – Limit the veto power to peace-keeping and enforcement issues.
  – Enhance early warning and threat assessment through the creation of a Security Assessment Staff based on existing United Nations staff and under the control of the Secretary-General.
  – Create an *ad hoc* military authority involved in each operation responding to an act of aggression as well as a United Nations Rapid Reaction Force.
  – ECOSOC functions should be split between an Economic Council and a Social Council, both forming an alliance for sustainable development through their close cooperation.

Social Council:
  – The Social Council, as a main organ of the United Nations,

would be responsible for supervising and integrating all United Nations agencies and programmes concerned with social issues.

Economic Council:
– The Economic Council, as another main organ of the United Nations, would coordinate monetary, financial and trade policies in addition to other economic issues such as employment creation and environmental protection, and provide guidance to the multiple activities of the United Nations system in these fields. The Bretton Woods institutions, Regional Economic Commissions, and development banks also play an important role in this respect.

United Nations Finances:
– Establish a working group to examine alternative sources of financing.

ANNEXE II

*AIDE-MÉMOIRE**

Review of the Role of the United Nations Trusteeship Council

The future of the Trusteeship Council is viewed within the wider context of United Nations revitalization and the will to enhance the Organization to better respond to the challenges of our times. The holistic vision which inspires the Charter remains the basis for action in this regard.

The balance pervading the Charter in terms of both fundamental principles and principal organs is as important today as it was fifty years ago. Established as a principal organ, the Trusteeship Council's essential attribute as depository of the principle of trust was at its basis and provides the single parameter relative to its future.

Application of the principle of trust through common responsibility proved to be a prototype of preventive diplomacy. It forestalled the conflict potential of differing claims of possession and ensured progressive development towards self-government or independence of the inhabitants of the trust territories.

'The absence of war and military conflict amongst States does not in itself ensure international peace and security,' warned the Heads of State and Government of the Security Council members in January 1992. *'The non-military sources of instability in the economic, social, humanitarian and ecological fields have become threats to peace and security.'* They emphasized that *'The United Nations membership as as whole, working through the appropriate bodies, needs to give the highest priority to the solution of these matters.'*

---

*This document, issued on 24 May 1996 by the Ministry of Foreign Affairs of Malta, was distributed to all Member States of the United Nations.

Conventions based on the application and consolidation of the principle of trust form part of the international community's response to this need. Conflict potential is pre-empted when certain areas or sectors, rather than left open to unrestrained competition, become the common responsibility of the international community as a whole. This awareness has led to the recognition of such concepts as common heritage, global commons and global concerns. Trust is their common denominator. The body most appropriate to coordinate these intertwined activities of trust is the Trusteeship Council.

In seeking to address sources of emerging instability, the Trusteeship Council can still prove to be the appropriate mechanism in certain instances. Apart from its role in the promotion and consolidation of the principles of trust and common responsibility, the Council's powers, in particular those in terms of Article 77.1 (c), remain.

Abolition of a principal organ affects the balance which pervades the Charter. It is not mere institutional pruning.

You will recall that Resolution 50/55 invites Member States to submit written comments on the future of the Trusteeship Council to the Secretary-General by May 31, 1996. The Government of Malta feels confident that your Government shares the view that, as depository of the principal of trust, the Trusteeship Council has an existing role which can be further consolidated.

COMMENTS OF THE GOVERNMENT OF MALTA

The Permanent Representative of Malta to the United Nations presents his compliments to the Secretary-General of the United Nations and has the honour to refer to the note verbale LA/COD/37 of December 27, 1995, inviting Member States to submit, by not later than 31st May 1996, written comments on the future of the Trusteeship Council in terms of the provisions of General Assembly resolution 50/55 of the 17th December 1995, entitled 'Review of the Role of the Trusteeship Council'.

The Permanent Representative of Malta has the honour to transmit hereunder the comments of the Government of Malta on the future of the Trusteeship Council.

REVITALIZING THE UNITED NATIONS

1.   Consolidation of peace, human rights, and sustainable development envision a world order based on solidarity, subsidiary and joint action.

2.   Freed from the grip of the cold war, the international community can go well beyond *détente*. Contemporary realities have breathed the will of Member States to revitalize the United Nations system. The common goal and aspiration is that of an enhanced United Nations that better responds to the challenges of our time in the interest of present and future generations.

3.   The forty-fifth session of the United Nations General Assembly was the threshold to this new era. Hopes and disappointments landmarked that session. They imposed a need to review the United Nations' ability to respond. Presiding that session, Prof. Guido de Marco held wide-ranging consultations on the subject with Member States and originated a number of initiatives to revitalize the United Nations and its principal organs.[1]

4.   On January 31, 1992, the Security Council held a historic meeting at the level of Heads of State and Government. The new challenges faced by the international community in the search for peace were noted. *'All member States expect the United Nations to play a central role at this crucial stage. The members of this Council stress the importance of strengthening and improving the United Nations to increase its effectiveness.'*[2]

5.   This urgent need was also the leitmotif of comprehensive reflection by Dr Boutros Boutros-Ghali, the United Nations' first post-cold war Secretary-General. His *Agenda for Peace* and *Agenda for Development* underlined the necessity to evaluate potentials and limitations of the United Nations system in the light of the new dynamics in international relations.

6.   These initiatives, together with other proposals from within and outside the system, have led to current broad-ranging discussion among Member States. The quest remains that of improving the United Nations' present capacities without losing sight of the fundamental principles on which the Organization was founded.

7.   Malta's proposal to review the role of the Trusteeship

---

[1] 'A Presidency with a Purpose', Ministry of Foreign Affairs, Malta, 1991.
[2] UN doc. S/23500, 31 Jan. 1992.

Council,[3] first launched by the President of the forty-fifth session of the United Nations General Asssembly,[4] was inspired and sustained by this comprehensive assessment of the Organization, current realities and nascent needs.

BALANCE PERVADES THE CHARTER

8. The United Nations was founded on the complete vision which emerged from the bitter experiences of war and conflict. This inspiring philosophy required a holistic institution – an Organization mandated with responsibility for the distinct yet interconnected areas of human activity and the safeguard of agreed and fundamental principles of international behaviour.

9. Balance pervades the Charter. Each principal organ projects principles vital to an international order based on peace, justice and freedom. Each is entrusted with specific responsibilities relative to the promotion of equity and the elimination of causes of conflict and tension. They must be viewed together within a perspective of equitable, balanced promotion and safeguard of the principles which each represents.

10. Institutional equilibrium is not the cause but the effect of this balance. The six principal organs are not mere organizational limbs, designed solely for the pragmatic distribution of work, which can be amputated at will.

11. Establishment of the Trusteeship Council as a principal organ of the United Nations was based on the in-built principles of trust and common responsibility. Like peace, security, equity, justice and the sovereign equality of States, these two fundamental principles cannot be bound or conditioned in their enunciation, acknowledgement or application by specific historical conditions or events.

12. The essential and innate value of principles is that they are lasting in time. Principles are the key to interpret events. Being indispensable in guiding international behaviour, they cannot be disposed of. Neither can those principal organs which, in a bal-

---

[3] 'Review of the Role of the Trusteeship Council' – UN doc. A150/142, 16 June 1995.

[4] Prof. Guido de Marco. Concluding Statement as President of 45-UNGA, 16 Sept. 1991 UN doc. A/45/PV.82.

anced manner, are entrusted by the Charter to promote and safeguard them.

13. *'With all the convulsions in global society, only one power is left that can impose order on incipient chaos: it is the power of principles transcending changing perceptions of expediency.'*[5]

NON-MILITARY SOURCES OF INSTABILITY

14. In the execution of its mandate during the past fifty years, the Trusteeship Council was guided by the underlying principles of trust and common responsibility. These provided the Council with the ability to address the peculiar nature of the different activities entrusted to it and a broad framework for the adoption of a consistent and coordinated approach.

15. The primary and basic objective of the trusteeship system was the furtherance of international peace and security through the activation of common responsibility. Placing territories under this system was unique. It forestalled the conflict potential of differing claims of possession. It was a tangible manifestation and application of the principles of trust and common responsibility by the international community. Benefit in the adoption of these principles was dual. Application proved to be a prototype of pre-emptive diplomacy and ensured the gradual and progressive development towards self-government or independence of the inhabitants of the territories.

16. Since then the concept of trust as a source of common responsibility of States has been further evolved by the international community. Conflict potential could be pre-empted if certain areas or sectors, rather than left to open, unrestrained competition, were to become the common responsibility of the international community as a whole. This awareness led to the recognition of such concepts as common heritage, global commons and global concerns. Trust is their common denominator. These concepts now form the basis of a number of conventions considered indispensable for international peace and security.

17. *'The absence of war and military conflict amongst States does not in itself ensure international peace and security,'* warned the Heads

---

[5] Statement by the Secretary-General at the 3046th meeting of the Security Council held at the level of Heads of State and Government on 31 January, 1992 – UN doc. S/PV.3046.

of State and Government of the Security Council members in January 1992. *'The non-military sources of instability in the economic, social, humanitarian and ecological fields have become threats to peace and security.'* They emphasized that *'The United Nations membership as a whole, working through the appropriate bodies, needs to give the highest priority to the solution of these matters.'*[6]

18.   Conventions based on the application and consolidation of the principle of trust form part of the international community's response to this need. The domain established in committing areas or sectors to the common responsibility of the international community as a whole is a new territory of trust. The agencies instituted by the conventions to manage and maintain these sectors are the administrators of these new trust territories. The body most appropriate to coordinate these intertwined activities of trust is the Trusteeship Council.

CURRENT MANDATE OF THE TRUSTEESHIP COUNCIL

19.   Since the end of the cold war, the United Nations has had to deal with new situations of a diverse and unpredictable nature. Given the different characteristics of these evolving situations, the United Nations should enhance rather than limit its options to act. It should not attentuate the potential envisaged by the foresight of the framers of the Charter. A revitalized United Nations, in seeking to address sources of instability, cannot dismantle a mechanism envisioned by the Charter which could be appropriate in certain situations.

20.   On 25 May, 1994, at its 1705th meeting, the Trusteeship Council adopted amendments to its rules of procedure.[7] Resolution T/RES/2200 (LXI) established that *'the Trusteeship Council shall meet as and where occasion may require, by decision of the Trusteeship Council, or by decision of its President, or at the request of a majority of its members, or at the request of the General Assembly, or at the request of the Security Council acting in pursuance of the relevant provisions of the Charter of the United Nations.'*

21.   In adopting this resolution without a vote the Council recognized that its mandate had not been exhausted. Apart from its role in the promotion and consolidation of the principles of trust

---

[6]   UN doc. S/23500, 31 January 1992.
[7]   UN doc. T/L. 1292 – 24 May 1994.

and common responsibility, the Council's powers, in particular those in terms of Article 77.1 (c) of the Charter, remain.

DEPOSITORY OF THE PRINCIPLE OF TRUST

22.   The Charter is the source of the United Nations' *raison d'être*, powers and potential. It was and remains the constant point of reference for Member States, particularly at a time when the Organization faces an array of concerns of an unprecedented nature. Abolition of a principal organ affects the balance of principles enunciated in the Charter. It is not a simple act of institutional pruning. The Trusteeship Council still has an effective role in the furtherance of the principle of trust which was at its inception as a principle organ.

23.   The Trusteeship Council's essential attribute as depository of the principle of trust was at its basis and provides the single parameter relative to its future.

24.   In 1967, Malta launched the concept of common heritage as applicable to the seabed, ocean floor and the subsoil thereof. The principle of trust is the keystone on which the concept of common heritage rests. Since then the principle of trust has been incorporated in other concepts in a number of conventions and agrreements. Its diffusion is a recognition of the common responsibility of the international community as a whole in the management and governance of certain areas.

25.   Human activity in these areas must be assessed within the wider context of its impact and consequences on the welfare and well-being of the whole family of nations. Common responsibility for these areas contributes towards international peace and security by pre-empting those tensions which would otherwise ensue from conflicting claims.

26.   The Trusteeship Council's current mandate can impress on the coordinated approach required in the application of the principle of trust in different areas. Malta's proposal to review the role of the Trusteeship Council was based on its essential attribute as depository of the principle of trust. Custodianship of this principle pre-empts tensions whilst securing the commonwealth of present and future generations.

27.   Progress has already been achieved in each distinct area where the principle of trust has been applied. Institutional mechanisms have been set up to implement the provisions of each of

the relevant conventions. Each maintains and manages the various and distinct areas. These existing agencies and bodies are and should remain the backbone and nervous system of worthy advance and rational implementation.

COORDINATION CORE

28. The distinct assignment of these bodies, however, needs a coordinating core. To better address potential institutional gaps and duplication of work, coordination is required in the wider inter-connective framework of trust and common responsibility. The international community recognizes the need for coordination. Curtailing duplication of effort and institutional fragmentation is cost-saving and brings to the fore other areas for which Member States bear common responsibilty. This co-ordinated approach is still lacking.

29. Malta believes that the Trusteeship Council is the focal point for such coordination. The mandate of this principal organ is based on the fundamental principles of trust and common responsibility. Like the other principal organs, the Council should continue to promote and safeguard the fundamental principles which are at the basis of its mandate. The application of the principles of trust and common responsibility in a number of international conventions makes their coordination the natural task of the Trusteeship Council.

30. For the above reasons, Malta believes that further consideration should be given to the Review of the Role of the Trusteeship Council.

The Permanent Representative of Malta to the United Nations avails himself of this opportunity to renew to the Secretary-General of the United Nations the assurances of his highest consideration.

BIBLIOGRAPHY

Allbright, Madeleine, 'America and the League of Nations: Lessons for today', Address to Woodrow Wilson International Centre for Scholars, 4 March 1994.

Asher, R. and Masin, E., *The World Bank since Bretton Woods*, 1973.

Balogh, T. *The Economics of Poverty*, Weidenfeld & Nicolson, London, 1965.

Bartolo, Michael, *Limitations of United Nations Technical Assistance*, ENDA-DAKAR, 1976.

Bertrand, Maurice, *L'ONU*, Paris, La Découverte, 1994.

————, Maurice, *Some Reflections on Reform of the United Nations*, Joint Inspection Unit, United Nations, Geneva, 1985 JIU/REP/85/9.

Borgese, Elisabeth Mann, *Ocean Governance and the United Nations*, Dalhousie University, 1995.

Boutros-Ghali, Boutros, *New Dimensions of Arms Regulation and Disarmament in the Post-Cold War Era*, United Nations, 1992.

Childers, Erskine, 'Never Again', Lecture to the Society for International Development, Amsterdam, 9 May 1991.

————, Erskine, 'Restoring the Role of the United Nations in Economic and Social Leadership', in *Malta Review of Foreign Affairs*, Special Issue, 1993.

————, E. and Urquhart, B., *A World in Need of Leadership*, Dag Hammarskjöld Foundation, 1990.

————, E. and Urquhart, B., *Towards a More Effective United Nations*, Dag Hammarskjöld Foundation, 1991.

————, E. and Urquhart, B., 'Reorganisation of the United Nations', February 1991 (unpublished).

————, E. and Urquhart, B., *Renewing the United Nations System*, Uppsala, Dag Hammarskjöld Foundation, 1994.

Claude, Inis, *Swords into Plowshares*, New York, Random House, 1964.

Commission on Global Governance, *A Call to Action – Summary of Our Global Neighbourhood*, Geneva, 1995.

Commission on Global Governance, *Our Global Neighbourhood*, Oxford University Press, Oxford, 1995.

de Marco, Guido, Ministry of Foreign Affairs, Malta, *Presidency with a Purpose*.

———, Guido, Statement to the Opening of the forty-fifth General Assembly, 18 September, 1990.

———, Guido, Statement at the forty-eighth session of the General Assembly, Malta Review of Foreign Affairs, 1 October 1993.

———, Guido, Statement at the forty-ninth session of the General Assembly, 30 September, 1994.

Dell, Sydney, 'Relations between the United Nations and the Bretton Woods Institutions', in *Development*, No.4, SID, Rome, 1989.

Evans, Gareth, *Cooperating for Peace – The Global Agenda for the 1990s and Beyond*, Allen & Unwin Pty. Ltd. St-Leonards (Australia), 1993.

Falk, Kim and Mendlovitz (eds.), *The United Nations and a Just World Order*, Westview Press, Boulder.

Ford Foundation, *Financing an Effective United Nations*, Independent Advisory Group on United Nations Financing (co-chairs Shejuro Ogata and Paul Volcker), 1993.

Gardner, Richard, *Sterling-Dollar Diplomacy in Current Perspective*, Columbia University Press, New York, 1980.

Gauci, Victor J., 'Malta and the Security Council', in *Malta Review of Foreign Affairs*, No.6, January 1995.

Goodrich, L., Hambro, E. *et al.*, *Charter of the United Nations*, New York, Columbia University Press, 1969.

Goulding, Marrack, 'The Evolution of United Nations Peacekeeping', in *International Affairs*, No.3, vol.69, July 1993.

Hall, Brian, 'Blue Helmets, Exporting Guns', *New York Times Magazine*, 2 January 1994.

Hayter, Teresa, *Aid as Imperialism*, Penguin Books, New York, 1971.

Heritage Foundation, *The United Nations: Its Problems and What to Do About Them*, September 1986.

Hudson, Michael, 'Epitaph for Bretton Woods', in *Journal of International Affairs*, No.2, vol.12, 1969.

Independent Working Group on the Future of the UN, *The United Nations in its Second Half Century*, Ford Foundation, New York, 1995.

Jackson, Sir, R. *A Study of the Capacity of the United Nations Development System*, 2 volumes, United Nations, Geneva, November, 1969.

Keenleyside, H. L., *International Aid: a Summary*, J. H. Heinemann Inc., New York, 1966.

Kirdar, U., *The Structure of United Nations Economic Aid to Underdeveloped Countries*, The Hague, 1966.

LeRoy, Bennett, *International Organizations: Principles and Issues*, Fifth Edition, Prentice Hall Inc., New Jersey, 1991.

Luard, Evan, *The United Nations: How It Works and What It Does*, New York, St Martin's Press, 1994.

Ministry of Foreign Affairs, Sweden, *Financial Management in International Organizations*, Stockholm, 1994.

Nerfin, Marc, 'The Future of the United Nations System', in *Development Dialogue*, No.1, 1985.

Nicholas, H. G., *The United Nations as a Political Institution*, London, Oxford University Press, 1971.

Nordic U.N. Project, *The Agencies at a Crossroads*, Report No.15, 1990.

——, *Financing the Multilateral System*, Report No.13, 1990.

——, *Perspectives on Multilateral Assistance*, Report No.10, 1989.

——, *Responding to Emergencies*, Report No.16, 1990.

Payer, Cheryl, *The Debt Trap: The IMF and the Third World*, Penguin Books, 1974.

Petrovsky, V., 'Preventive Diplomacy and Conflict Resolution: Redefining the Role of the United Nations', Speech, Graz, Austria, June 1993.

PGA, 'Towards a Global Security System for the 21st Century: a Submission to the Secretary-General of the United Nations', in *PGA Newsletter*, June 1993, pp.6–7.

Prebisch, Raul, *Towards a Global Strategy of Development*: United Nations, New York, 1968.

Preston Baratta, Joseph, *Strengthening the United Nations*, New York, Greenwood Press, 1987.

Renninger, John, 'Improving the UN System', in *Journal of Development Planning*, No.17, 1987, pp.85–111.

Scott, George, *The Rise and Fall of the League of Nations*, Hutchinson & Co Ltd., London, 1973.

Singer, Hans, *International Development: Growth and Change*, McGraw-Hill, New York, 1964.

Society for International Development, *The United Nations and the Bretton Woods Institutions: New Challenges for the 21st Century*, Bretton Woods N.H., September 1993.

South Centre, *For a Strong and Democratic United Nations – A South Perspective on Reform*, Geneva, 1996.

Spiers, R., 'United Nations Secretariat Reform', draft of 2 May 1991.

Spiry, Emmanuel, 'La réforme des institutions onusiennes: perspectives et prospectives (1985–1995)', *Studia Diplomatica*, vol.XLVIII, 1995, No.3, pp.63–95.

Stanley Foundation, *State of the United Nations: Decline or Regeneration in the Next Fifty Years*, 1994.

Stassen, Harold, *United Nations: A Working Paper for Restructuring*, Minneapolis, Lerner Pub., 1994.

BIBLIOGRAPHY

UNDP, *Human Development Report 1992*, Oxford University Press, Oxford.

———, *Human Development Report 1994*, Oxford University Press, Oxford.

United Nations, Charter.

———, *A New United Nations Structure for Global Economic Cooperation*, E/AC.62/9, 1975.

———, *Comprehensive Review of the Whole Question of Peace-Keeping Operations in All Their Aspects*, A/48/173, May 1993 (Special Committee on Peace-Keeping Operations).

———, *Implementation of the Recommendations Contained in 'An Agenda for Peace'*, A/47/965 5/25944, June 1993.

———, *Towards Greater Order, Coherence and Coordination in the United Nations*, E/5491, 30 April 1994.

———, *Agenda for Development*, A/48/935, 6 May 1994.

Urquhart, Brian, 'For a UN Volunteer Military Force', in *The New York Review of Books*, 10 June 1993, pp.3–4.

———, B., *Tomorrow's United Nations*, Dag Hammarskjöld Foundation, 1990.

Waters, Maurice, *The United Nations*, The MacMillan Company, New York, 1967.

INDEX

T - #0038 - 270225 - C0 - 216/138/11 [13] - CB - 9780710305589 - Gloss Lamination